The Mansfields of Co. Kildare

T0002887

Maynooth Studies in Local History

SERIES EDITOR Michael Potterton

You are reading one of the six volumes in the Maynooth Studies in Local History (MSLH) series for 2023. A benefit of being the editor of this series is the early opportunity to read a very wide variety of bite-sized histories covering events and activities from the magnificent to the outrageous in every nook and cranny of this remarkable island. This year's offerings take us from Bronze Age burials in west Kerry to a three-year dairy war in 1930s east Donegal, via an entrepreneur extraordinaire from late Georgian Cork, a revelatory survey of dire poverty in pre-Famine Westmeath, a century of exclusive terrace-life in colourful Tralee and the complex social networks of a family of Francophile Catholic landed gentry from Kildare. Together, these six studies take us on an astonishing journey on which we encounter smugglers, umbrella makers, lifelike automata, difficult marriage- and education choices, resolute defiance, agrarian violence, rapidly changing religious and political landscapes and a petition to have a region transferred from one nation to another.

These half-a-dozen volumes show how the 'local' focus of a *local history* can range from an individual person (Marsden Haddock) to a family (the Mansfields), a street (Day Place), a village (Portmagee), a county (Donegal and Westmeath) and beyond. The six authors have taken their stories from relative obscurity to centre stage. Denis Casey now joins Terence Dooley as one of only two people to have published three volumes in this series (though they are set to be joined by a third in 2024!).

This year in the Department of History at Maynooth University we are celebrating seventy years of excellence in teaching, research and publication (1953–2023) and we are especially delighted to be relaunching our enormously successful MA in Local History. Theses from this programme have traditionally provided the backbone of the MSLH series and we look forward to another rich crop in the years to come.

Whether you ask Alexa, ChatGPT or Raymond Gillespie, there is no doubting that Local History is valuable and significant. AI has evolved considerably since I grew up on a dairy farm in south Co. Meath and it is sure to play an increasing role in the research, writing and dissemination of local history. As with so many new technologies, of course, the greatest challenge is perhaps going to be maximizing the potential of Artificial Intelligence without compromising the integrity of the results.

Maynooth Studies in Local History: Number 165

The Mansfields of Co. Kildare: a Franco-Irish Catholic elite family and their networks, 1870–1915

Fergus P. Murphy

FOUR COURTS PRESS

Set in 11.5pt on 13.5pt Bembo by
Carrigboy Typesetting Services for
FOUR COURTS PRESS LTD
7 Malpas Street, Dublin 8, Ireland
www.fourcourtspress.ie
and in North America for
FOUR COURTS PRESS
c/o IPG, 814 N Franklin Street, Chicago, IL 60610

© Fergus P. Murphy and Four Courts Press 2023

ISBN 978-1-80151-098-1

All rights reserved. Without limiting the rights under
copyright reserved alone, no part of this publication may
be reproduced, stored in or introduced into a retrieval system,
or transmitted, in any form or by any means (electronic,
mechanical, photocopying, recording or otherwise), without
the prior written permission of both the copyright
owner and the above publisher of this book.

Printed in Ireland
by SprintPrint, Dublin

Contents

Acknowledgments   7
Introduction   8
1   The Mansfield family, estate and marriage networks   14
2   Catholic elite networks in Ireland through the lens of
    George and Alice Mansfield   33
3   The impact of adding a bi-national dimension to an Irish
    Catholic elite network   48
Conclusion   62
Appendices   65
Notes   72

FIGURES

1   Mansfield family pedigree, 1642–1967   15
2   Morristown Lattin House, Co. Kildare   16
3   Outline map of Co. Kildare, 1853   18
4   George Mansfield   19
5   Alice Mansfield   21
6   Eustace and Henry Mansfield   22
7   Intermarriage within Mansfield network   25
8   Margaret Mansfield   27
9   Henry Lattin Mansfield   31
10   Geographic spread of Mansfield network in Ireland, 1879–89   34
11   Mansfield family core network   35
12   Family locations for Mansfield core network   36
13   Ballinkeele House, Enniscorthy, Co. Wexford   41
14   GPL Mansfield and brothers in the Kildare Hunt   45
15   Mansfield family location, 1877–87   50
16   Map view of Mansfield family locations in France, 1877–87   50
17   Days per location for five Mansfield trips to France, 1877–87   51
18   Division of time across locations outside Ireland, 1877–87   53
19   Frequency of diary mentions of families while in France   53

20 Maternal kin connections for Alice Mansfield   58
21 Influence of Alice and George on family network   61

TABLES
1   Mansfield core social network   35
2   French core social network, 1877–87   54

Acknowledgments

There are a number of people to whom I would like to express my gratitude for their assistance in researching, writing and preparing this publication. First, I would like to thank all the staff at the University of Limerick and the Glucksman Library; in particular, Dr Rachel Murphy, who was my supervisor for the dissertation upon which this publication is based, and Dr Ciara Breathnach. To the many others who assisted me and offered advice during my research, Dr Martin O'Donoghue, Dr Richard Kirwan and Dr Roberto Mazzo as well as Pattie Punch. My thanks are also due to the archivists and librarians at the National Library of Ireland in Kildare Street, Dublin, and the National Archives, Bishop Street, Dublin, who assisted me during my research. I would also like to acknowledge and thank Kevin Murphy at Kildare Local Studies & Archives Collections for allowing me to use some family photographs from their George Mansfield Photographic Archive. A special word of gratitude is due to Dr Michael Potterton, the series editor, for his advice and guidance and for including this study in the series.

I would like to spare a thought for the people who have been the focus of much of my research, the Mansfield family, and who, in spirit, have been somewhat present throughout that period. I have read their correspondence and diaries with intrigue, as if I was living their lives at times.

Finally, I am especially thankful to all of my family for their never-ending support and, in particular, to Killian and Antoine for their patience while I became absorbed with this project. This work is dedicated to them and my inspirational and supportive parents.

Introduction

This study builds upon existing scholarship for Catholic landed gentry in Ireland in the late nineteenth and early twentieth centuries. First, it develops insights into Catholic elite social and marriage networks through a microstudy of the Franco-Irish Mansfield family in Co. Kildare, from 1870 to 1915, and second, it provides an understanding of the structure, origins and significance of both Irish and French networks to this bi-national family. While examining these, it also discusses aspects of religion, class, nationality and language within those networks. In scoping the field of history, John Tosh identifies several branches of specialization for history – political, economic, social, world and local. The study is written in the context of studies on history of the family, which is typically considered to be a sub-branch of social history, and falls within the field of local history. Tosh splits social history into two categories, the history of social problems and the history of everyday life.[1] This study identifies primarily with the latter. He also describes local history as 'a kind of in-depth microcosmic social history', as breathing 'life into abstractions' and by virtue of its focus on two localities – Co. Kildare and south-west France – the study also helps to promote a better understanding of historic elite communities therein.[2] I would also like the acknowledge and thank Kevin Murphy at Kildare Local Studies & Archives Collection for allowing me to use some family photographs from their George Mansfield Photographic Archive.

The study also fits within the history of Catholic landed elite families in Ireland and, to a lesser extent, in France in the late nineteenth and early twentieth century. Following Catholic emancipation and a gradual end to the Penal Laws in the late 1820s, the Catholic people of Ireland were in a much stronger position to be socially mobile. This volume provides a case study for examining just how much of a social divide still existed between elite Protestants and Catholics in the period 1870–1915, through the lens of the Mansfield family. Much work has been produced on landed estates in Ireland, primarily on estates in the possession of Protestant landed gentry. Scholars such as Terence Dooley, Paddy Duffy, Karen Harvey, Art Kavanagh and William Vaughan have nevertheless produced work on Catholic landed estates while Turtle Bunbury, Con Costello and Emma Lyons have focused specifically on Co. Kildare.[3] The aim of this study is to add to that work by looking at the origins of the Mansfield estate, how their Co. Kildare land was acquired, how they came to be landed elite and examines how they kept their status through the eighteenth-century Penal-Law period. It questions how important their Catholic religion was to them. Dooley specifically states that,

> regardless of religion, social standing or estate size, all landlords shared the same cultural values and to varying extents ... exercised the same social, political and economic powers ... conferred by landownership in their respective localities,[4]

and the Mansfield family microstudy tests that statement.

During the period under consideration (1870–1915), a Catholic elite education structure started to form in Ireland with schools such as Clongowes Wood and Blackrock College. Nevertheless, elites such as the Mansfield family followed the long tradition of Irish Protestants and Catholics, sending their children abroad to schools in England, France, Belgium and elsewhere. The study builds upon existing scholarship on Catholic elite and transnational education, such as the work of Ciaran O'Neill, by trying to understand why the Mansfield family made this choice and if that played into their social and marriage network.[5] Like many members of the landed elite of the time, the Mansfields entertained in their big house, Morristown Lattin, and the microstudy provides insights into the entertainment practices of a Catholic elite family in building its social network. As such, it questions the existing historiography on big-house entertainment practices, particularly the aforementioned work of Dooley and that of Maeve O'Riordan.[6] While the role of women in building elite social networks is an area of family and social history that has been researched and written about by authors such as O'Riordan for Ireland and Elizabeth MacKnight for France, there is little or no work done to date on the role of women in building networks associated with a bi-national and bilingual family.[7] As a New-York-born, Paris-bred elite lady, the analysis of Alice Mansfield's diary, and the role that she played in the Mansfield social network in Ireland and France, provides a microstudy that fits within this historiography, allowing the study to highlight the effect of the French connection on those social networks and thus aims to reduce that gap.

The study leans on multiple primary sources, with the Mansfield family papers, held at the National Library of Ireland, as the principal one. Newspapers have also been used in understanding their social networks and the associated activities, providing additional context such as religion or class, where the family papers may provide only a name. Land records have been used in tandem with newspapers to identify some of the families within the Mansfields' network and their position in society. These include Griffith's Valuation for Co. Kildare and the 1876 Return of Owners of Land of One Acre in Ireland.[8] Research was also conducted within school archives to support the analysis of their role within the family's networks. Within the family papers, extensive use has been made of diaries and, to a lesser extent, personal correspondence as well as wills and marriage settlements. The principal source document underpinning much of the analysis has been Alice's manuscript diary from 12 October 1877, the year of her marriage, to 2 May 1887, five months short of ten years.[9] The family papers also contain a diary for Alice from 1846, when she was a young girl, to 1876 and then several other diaries up to 1932, two years prior to her death, with a gap from 1897 to 1899. Thus, the ten-year period under consideration is but a snapshot and for a very specific phase of her life, one during which she had just married George, emigrated to Ireland and started a family, at the end of which she was 41 years old. The papers also contain extensive diaries for George, which are referenced to a much lesser extent.

Alice's diary is a ruby-coloured soft-bound journal with gilded lines around the edge of the cover page and contains thirty-six pages, with entries on both sides. It measures 19cm by 12cm, roughly equivalent to A5. It was purchased in Paris. It is notable that two pages have been torn from the back of the diary, corresponding with the time of her life when one of her sons died at home. All diary entries for the ten-year period were written in French, as was much of the personal correspondence in the family papers. For the purposes of this study, the original handwritten diary was consulted, transcribed and translated for the ten years. This represents a total of 435 entries and more than 8,400 words. Appendices below show sample pages from the diary and associated transcription and translation. The diary entries are typically in note form, often with abbreviations, and the handwriting was for the most part legible, once the style was understood. The diary was the principal source used in constructing and analysing a view of the Mansfield social network.

Following transcription and translation, Alice's diary was parsed with a view to extracting family names, frequency of mention of the same, activities, locations and any indication of religion or class. The frequency of mention of any one family or connection has been used as a proxy to represent the time spent with that family. Any gaps were completed, where possible, by triangulation using the previously mentioned primary sources. It was, however, not possible to fill all of the gaps, particularly for families in France. Such a manual process has its complexities; for example, trying to determine whether Mr Kane, as mentioned by Alice, was one and the same person as Captain Kane or whether perhaps the correct spelling was Cane, in which case it could be a different person and family. Despite this challenge for a small number of families in the network, the methodology allowed for the creation of a database that provides an accurate representation of the Mansfield social network. The same process was used for both Ireland and France, albeit with some gaps remaining in the French network. With this data, it was also possible to map the locations visited geographically across the ten-year period in both countries. For Ireland, newspapers and census records were particularly useful in providing context to confirm class and religion, as well as the activities upon which they constructed their social network, in addition to confirming location in some instances. Correspondence within the Mansfield papers, *Burke's landed gentry of Ireland, Burke's peerage* and birth, marriage and death registrations were key sources in completing the genealogy for many of the families in their family network, which enabled an understanding of the role of intermarriage. Finally, the records for the County Kildare Archaeological Society and the County Kildare Online Electronic History Journal were referenced numerous times in completing the picture.[10] French-language primary sources including newspapers, genealogy records and civil records in addition to secondary sources for landed gentry were used in analysing the French network.[11]

There is a wide variance of opinion on the use of the diary as a primary source. When comparing some of Alice's notes with other sources such as civil records or newspaper accounts, the diary appears to be accurate, although it is not especially descriptive. She wrote about her own and her family's activities on a regular basis – at times daily and, at other times, there are gaps of several weeks. It is likely that this is for reasons other than being selective in what she records. Apart from the time of her marriage and subsequent arrival in Ireland, it was unusual for Alice to record personal feelings, and she never expresses emotion following childbirth or infant death. Nevertheless, she does give strong opinions on a number of occasions. It would thus appear that Alice kept her diaries to create a record and freeze time, one of the four typical functions of a diary as outlined by Philippe Lejeune – self-expression, reflection, to freeze time and for the pleasure of writing. Despite the non-descriptive style and difficulty with identifying where some of the people named fit within their network, or other information about them, Alice's diary provides an abundance of information about her family and their networks in Ireland and France over the ten-year period.

The study adds to existing scholarship on Catholic elite networks by answering a number of questions, such as who did George and Alice Mansfield socialize with for the first ten years of their 1877 marriage? Was their network exclusively Catholic, or was it a function of their class more than their religion? To what extent was their network made up of kin relations and did paternal or maternal kin prevail?[12] As a bi-national family, how much time did they spend in France, was it unusual and how significant was this French connection to their social network? Which partner was the most influential on the network in Ireland, and in France? Was it possible for Alice to build her own local network in Ireland or did she rely primarily on that of her Irish husband? Did Alice comply with the stereotypical elite woman as advanced by MacKnight, whereby being a good hostess was a 'serious ambition for upper-class women'?[13] As a bilingual family, the study questions whether Alice's language skills, or possible lack thereof, had any impact on building and maintaining their social network in Ireland. It also questions what the intersection was between their social and marriage networks, how important religion was in that context, what role kin played and was their behaviour typical of Catholic elite.

The first chapter covers the origins of the family and their estate, inheritance behaviour and marriage strategies for elite families and a discussion of intermarriage within the Mansfield social network. It concludes by examining their choice of education for their sons and the relationship between the latter and their social network and marriage choices. The second chapter covers kinship, public and sporting networks, their intersection and the relative importance of religion and class in that context. It also addresses the role of women in those networks through the eyes of Alice and her diary. The third chapter considers how a bi-national family such as the Mansfields spent their time geographically to maintain social networks in both Ireland and France. It also looks specifically at their social networks in France through a religion and class lens, the intersection with their network in Ireland and the relative importance of maternal and paternal kin in both countries.

1. The Mansfield family, estate and marriage networks

The Mansfield family, who in 1870 resided at Morristown Lattin in the townland of Morristown Upper in Co. Kildare, were apparently present in Ireland since the twelfth-century Anglo-Norman invasion when Sir Rodulphus Mansfield came from Nottinghamshire.[1] It is possible that they were Anglo-Normans, given the variations of the family name, which according to Turtle Bunbury was originally 'de Mandeville'.[2] It is reported that Rodulphus was granted estates in counties Armagh, Derry, Waterford, Cork and Limerick, and that he settled in Killongford and Ballinamultina, Co. Waterford. These estates appear to have remained in the family up to the time of his descendant, Walter Mansfield, b. 1622 (the year in which the family pedigree in fig. 1 begins).[3]

Walter took part in the Irish Rebellion in 1641 as a result of which the Irish Catholic clergy and gentry, including the Mansfields, formed the Catholic Confederation and were close to taking control of the country.[4] However, following the 1649–50 Cromwellian campaign in Ireland, Walter Mansfield's estate was confiscated because of his part on the Catholic side of the wars, and he was transplanted, like many others, to Connacht in 1653–4.[5] After the Restoration in 1660 when Charles II returned to the throne, Walter recovered part of the Ballinamultina estate, which was the only part of the once-extensive estates to remain within the family. Walter married Helen Power, and their son Richard fought with the army of Catholic James II in Ireland against William of Orange, culminating in the defeat of James II at the Battle of the Boyne in 1690.[6]

Despite having lost the majority of their property, the Mansfield family remained Catholic and succeeded, whether by chance or by design, in expanding their estates during the eighteenth century through marriage with wealthy and prominent families. This was despite the Penal Laws, whereby the eldest son was required to

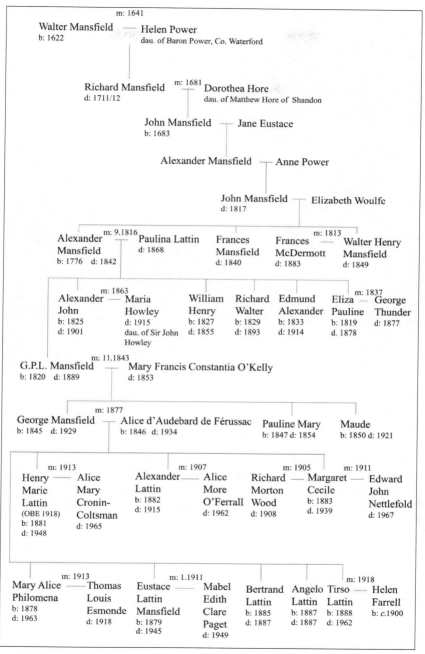

1. Mansfield family pedigree, 1642–1967 (sources: NLI, Mansfield Papers, Collection list no. 77; *Burke's Irish family records* (London, 1977), pp 784–5)

2. Morristown Lattin House, Co. Kildare
(source: Fonsie Mealy Auctioneers (www.fonsiemealy.ie), 5 Mar. 2019)

conform to the Church of Ireland if he was to inherit the whole estate, which was a move that was intended to break up Catholic estates by ending primogeniture and enforcing gavelkind.[7] How they may have achieved this during the Penal-Law period is an interesting question that deserves some consideration, particularly because of the decline in Catholic landholding during the eighteenth century from approximately 14 per cent in 1703 to 5 per cent in 1776.[8] Nevertheless, there were 'Catholic gentry families who prospered' during that period, according to Harvey who, in writing about the Catholic Bellew estate in Co. Galway, notes that there were 'instances of successful circumvention, through successful litigation; judicious use of trustees or discovery by collusion, that is, a friendly Protestant bringing action to forestall a genuine discovery' or the 'practice of obtaining a "Protestant friend" or even hiring one as a professional discoverer to facilitate land conveyancing', citing the dealings of the

Bellews with the Protestant McCartans.[9] In researching the Lattin family during the eighteenth century and their Co. Kildare estates, Lyons discovered that they were 'one such Catholic family who used collusive tactics to retain their landed property' and 'actually managed to increase their land holdings by having a "friendly" Protestant purchase land in trust for them or by manipulating the use of long leases ... to circumvent the statutes'.[10]

Four generations later, the family was firmly established in Co. Kildare when, in 1817, Alexander married Paulina Lattin, the only child of Patrick Lattin and heiress of Lattin's Morristown estate in Co. Kildare.[11] The Lattin family were Catholic and originally from France. One branch of the family appears to have been granted lands in Co. Kildare by King John (1199–1216), which they managed to retain during the Penal-Law period. In 1692, just three years prior to the first penal laws, they built the big house on the estate known as Morristown Lattin (fig. 2).

Patrick Lattin was born at Morristown Lattin in 1762 and the family lived there up until his death in 1836 (although he actually died in his Parisian home), at which point it passed into the hands of Paulina Lattin and her husband Alexander Mansfield.[12] As an only child, Paulina appears to have been a very wealthy heiress, given that in 1814 her parents entered into a conveyance concerning property at Ballyrobbin in Waterford from which more than £5,000 was to be raised for Paulina, which was to be given to her at the age of 21 or upon her marriage.[13]

The eldest son of Alexander and Paulina, George Patrick Lattin (GPL) Mansfield, was born in 1820 and succeeded to the Mansfield estate and the Morristown Lattin house in Co. Kildare (by right of his mother), when his father died in 1842. In 1843 GPL married Mary Bourke O'Kelly, another Catholic, who was co-heiress of the estate left by her father George Bourke O'Kelly, apparently a wealthy sugar planter in the Virgin Islands, and her mother, Mary de Pentheny. Edmund de Pentheny Bourke O'Kelly, Mary Mansfield's brother, succeeded to part of the Barretstown estate, adjacent to Morristown Lattin in Co. Kildare (fig. 3). The Barretstown estate covered Barretstown, Clongorey, Blacktrench and Tankards Garden townlands.[14] GPL and Mary Mansfield had three children before Mary died young, in 1853. GPL continued to live at Morristown Lattin with

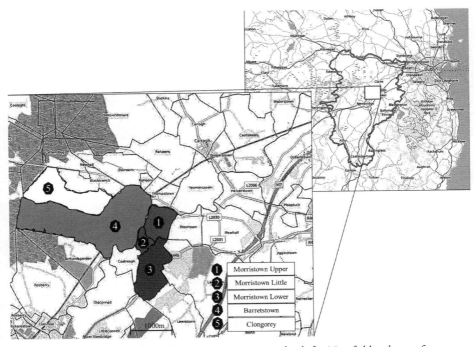

3. Outline map of Co. Kildare zooming in on townlands for Mansfield and part of Barretstown estates, 1853 (sources: OpenStreetMap (www.openstreetmap.ie); Irish Townlands (www.townlands.ie), 12 Apr. 2019)

his three children and was clearly a well-respected man in the county; a JP and a DL for Co. Kildare in 1874 as well as high sheriff in 1851. In 1853, at the time of Griffith's Valuation for Co. Kildare, GPL and his mother Paulina owned 3,550 acres in that county and were landlords to ninety-seven tenants. Figure 3 shows three of the townlands in which the Co. Kildare estate owned by GPL and his mother Paulina in 1853 was situated – Morristown Upper, Morristown Little and Morristown Lower.[15] Paulina died in 1868 and by 1876 there were 4,057 acres in the name of GPL, situating him within the top fifteen landowners in the county.[16] GPL was also the principal trustee for the neighbouring 2,500-acre O'Kelly estate at Clongorey townland (fig. 3), the same Catholic O'Kelly family from which his wife Mary was descended, up until his death in 1889.[17]

GPL and Mary's eldest child, George, who, along with his wife Alice, are the focus of this study, was born in 1845 and educated at

4. George Mansfield (source: Costello, *A class apart* (2005))

Stonyhurst, a Catholic boarding school in Lancashire, England. He succeeded to the Mansfield estate and followed in his father's footsteps as a JP and DL for Co. Kildare, as well as being the county's high sheriff in 1874.

As Catholic landed elites, the Mansfield family appear to have been good landlords, who were sympathetic to the plight of their less-well-off tenants. In Mary Ryan's thesis on the Clongorey evictions, when writing about GPL, she states that

> Fr Kinsella attended to Mr Mansfield before he died in 1889. He recalled in his evidence to the Evicted Tenants Commission that at one of these meetings, Mr Mansfield told him of his regret at the treatment that the tenants were suffering at the hands of the agent Ruttledge, on the instructions of Matthew Maher, one of the trustees of the estate. He hoped on his recovery to resume principal trusteeship and try to help the tenants.[18]

Notwithstanding the reality that obituaries generally tended to be positive and a little prosaic, the 1929 *Leinster Leader* obituary to George gives a similar impression of considered and fair landlords, where it states 'the welfare of his tenants, past and present, was always a foremost consideration with him, and his intimate knowledge and concern in their varying fortunes revealed how closely he regarded their interests and his own as interwoven'.[19] Further evidence of this is seen from the formal addresses on the occasion of the garden party hosted by the Mansfield family, for about two hundred of their tenants, on the Morristown Lattin demesne shortly after George and Alice's 1877 marriage in Paris, as recognition for gifts offered by the tenants. Laurence Duggan, who spoke on behalf of the tenants, stated 'The Tenantry have always found in the honour of the Mansfields a security stronger than any law could give' and George responded with a long speech that gives the impression of a remarkably healthy relationship between landlord and tenant, including statements such as

> I need not tell you what pleasure it gives me to see around me so many old and valued friends ... I feel so much touched by the kind manner in which you refer to the good feelings which have always existed between landlord and tenants on the Mansfield estates, and it shall be my constant endeavour to follow the example of my ancestors and above all to put in practice the lessons which my father's useful and devoted life has placed before me ... that to live constantly amongst you all doing my best to fulfil the duties of my portions is my most fervent wish.[20]

Such a reputation was no doubt well-earned, however it is important to put this in context and note that Dooley states 'there is ample evidence of tenants being entertained by the landlord on the demesne ... between the mid-1850s and the late 1870s'. He calls it '"good PR" for the tenants to ... express congratulations ... on his son getting married' and notes that it was 'traditional for the landlord, in return, to reward his tenants' support with a dinner or a luncheon', citing instances from the Clonbrock estate in Co. Galway and Brabazon estate in Co. Wicklow, both examples of Protestant landlords.[21]

Nevertheless, whether 'good PR' or not, the relationship referred to by George in his address and the way the Mansfield family managed their tenants appears to be one of the factors that ensured

5. Alice Mansfield (source: George Mansfield Photographic Archive, Kildare Local Studies & Archives Collections)

the Mansfield estate remained largely intact throughout the Land War that was to follow a few years later, while other surrounding estates, such as the aforementioned Clongorey estate, from 1883, were struggling and evicting tenants. As O'Neill states, however, 'owning such an extraordinary amount of land separated these families from the majority of Irish Catholics and placed them in an uncomfortable position, straddling the mostly non-Catholic landed gentry and their own tenants and co-religionists'. The Mansfields appear to have managed the situation well considering O'Neill's view that being 'resident on their land' most of the time and having a 'shared faith' that put them 'physically ... closer to their tenants than was usually

6. Eustace and Henry Mansfield (source: George Mansfield Photographic Archive, Kildare Local Studies & Archives Collections)

the case with their Protestant peers' was risky, citing the Considine family in Pallas Green, Co. Limerick, as an example of one that felt 'the wrath of their tenantry' in 1881.[22] Harvey, on the other hand, advances that 'amicable landlord–tenant relations in eighteenth-century Galway' between Catholic landlords and their Catholic tenants may actually have been as a result of the fact that they 'were not absentee landlords, but resided on their estates'.[23]

George's will dating from 1910 gives the impression of a modest, considerate man, wherein he states 'I wish to be buried in the new cemetery Caragh without pomp or expense and should I die abroad I do not wish my body brought back to Ireland'.[24] The 1901 census return shows the Mansfield family employing ten servants in Morristown Lattin, all Catholic, all Irish and six from Co. Kildare.[25] According to Dooley, 'landlords preferred to "import" their servants' and thus 'big houses were not of great economic benefit to locals seeking employment'. Indeed, of the one hundred sample houses that Dooley analysed (of which only 8 per cent were Catholic-owned), 61 per cent of the servants were Irish-born and only 14 per cent locally born. However, it is important to take religion into account and, as Dooley points out, 'there was an overall propensity by Protestant landlords to employ Protestant' servants and 'a similar propensity amongst Catholic landlords to employ Catholic servants', and the Mansfield family as an example tallies with this statement.[26] Nonetheless, the roster of servants clearly supports the impression given by George's obituary of an interest in local people and shows that the Mansfield family were perhaps somewhat unusual by virtue of the extent with which they integrated into the local community, possibly influenced by the fact that they were Catholic.

In 1877, George married Alice d'Audebard de Férussac (fig. 5) in Paris. Born in New York, she was the eldest daughter of Baron d'Audebard de Férussac from Paris, and Alice Thorn, an American opera singer from New York.[27] From Alice's 1934 obituary in the *Evening Herald*, it is clear that she was from a very noble background. Her American maternal grandfather 'was a prominent social figure' in the early nineteenth century, residing between 'his magnificent residence at 16th St. and Fifth Av. [*sic*] ... his country estate at Troy, New York' and 'a beautiful chateau in Paris. His three daughters ... married into the French nobility'. As a child, Alice 'was a welcome visitor to the Palace of the Empress Eugenie' and 'attended the famous balls and entertainment given by the Emperor Napoleon III and his beautiful wife'.[28] George and Alice had eight children, six sons and two daughters, all but one born at Morristown Lattin – Mary in 1878, Eustace Lattin in 1879, Henry Marie Lattin in 1881 (fig. 6), Alexander Lattin in 1882, Marguerite in 1883 in France, Bertrand Lattin in 1885, Angelo in 1887 and Tirso in 1888.[29] The naming that George and Alice adopted for their children is an example of a practice that, according to Mark Rothery, is 'a telling indicator of cultures of kinship, signifying affection and belonging', whereby all of their sons were given their paternal grandmother's maiden name, Lattin, as their second Christian name.[30] George lived all his life at Morristown Lattin and died there in 1929 of 'chronic arthritis and cardiac asthma', while Alice lived out her final years close to her eldest daughter, Mary, in Rathgar, Dublin, where she died in 1934 of pneumonia.[31]

From Alice's diary and the 1901 and 1911 census returns, it would appear that there were three generations of the Mansfield family living together in Morristown Lattin at certain stages of the family lifecycle: Alice's father-in-law (GPL), GPL's brother, Edmund, George's sister, Maude, and Alice, George and their growing family, along with a 21-year-old More O'Ferrall cousin and ten servants.[32] From a household structure perspective, the Mansfield family can be considered to have been a stem family household or a *famille souche*, as first defined by Frederic Le Play to be one made up of grandparents, parents and their children, essentially three generations of the patriarchal family under one roof.[33] Based on research on landed gentry families in Northern Ireland, Amanda Shanks states that they exhibited two important norms of inheritance, first that their priority was to prevent the division of their property and second that of primogeniture as the preferred mode of inheritance. Indeed, Shanks maintains that the stem-family structure was not as much about who resided in the house as it was the result of favouring primogeniture for inheritance.[34] The Mansfield family are a reflection of those norms for several generations, at least up to George as the head of the family.

Marriage strategies were also important to landed elite families for the future of their children but also for the future of their estates and, as a strategy, intermarriage was notable among Catholic landed families in Ireland. Taking this a step further, O'Neill states that a 'local marriage pattern [was] replicated among Irish Catholic families', whereby there was a 'tendency to marry not only within the landed class but … into families which are relatively close'.[35] In this latter regard, George and Alice and their children were atypical whereas the previous generation, GPL Mansfield, was certainly an example of this pattern, notably with the Mansfield-O'Kelly connection. Coupled with class and locality, kinship is an important factor to consider and intermarriage among kin was a notable characteristic of the Catholic families that formed part of the Mansfield social network, something

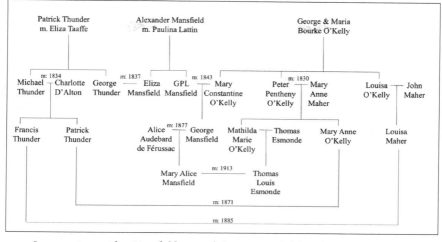

7. Intermarriage within Mansfield network (sources: *Burke's landed gentry of Ireland*; NLI, Mansfield Papers; General Register Office)

that is very evident from Alice's diary and the Mansfield family papers. The family connections that made up much of the Mansfield social network that are discussed later came about as a result in many cases of several generations of intermarriage among Catholics that were their kin. Based on nineteenth-century research for England, it would appear that this was not unusual for elite families there either, albeit Protestant in that case.[36] The reason advanced by O'Neill for Catholic elite families was that land was of utmost importance and by marrying with 'families they knew well and had relied upon as neighbours' through centuries of upheaval and threat, they were protecting their estates, preferring to prioritize multiple generations of landownership over a single-generation marriage relationship.[37]

As can be seen in figure 7, GPL Mansfield married into the O'Kelly family and, in the same generation, GPL's sister-in-law, Louisa O'Kelly, married John Maher and his brother-in-law, Peter Pentheny O'Kelly, married John's sister, Mary Anne Maher.[38] A generation later, intermarriage among cousins becomes a feature when Thomas Esmonde married Peter Pentheny's daughter, Mathilda Marie O'Kelly. Their son, Thomas Louis, married George and Alice's eldest daughter, Mary Alice Mansfield, in 1913. In referring to Sabean and Johnson, Rothery states that, from the mid-eighteenth century, for European nobility, 'old lineage models' of family relationships evolved due to growth in social equality to a model whereby 'cousin marriage became increasingly acceptable'.[39] In England, 'marriages between first cousins ... were typical of ... educated upper-middle class' during the nineteenth century, and the Esmonde-Mansfield marriage is one such example of Catholic Irish gentry following this trend.[40] Two further examples of intermarriage among Catholic kin within the Mansfield core network are the nephew of GPL's sister, Eliza and George Thunder, a Patrick Thunder, and Mary Anne O'Kelly in 1871, and George and Alice's son, Alexander, and Alice More O'Ferrall.

In general, as Duffy states, the Protestant 'gentry had a real horror of intermarriage with Catholics of any hue' and this lasted well into the late nineteenth century.[41] As such, it may be that Catholic gentry like the Mansfield family felt the same 'horror', thus leaving units like the Mansfield family with little or no choice but to marry within their own religion. It is interesting to note that, while the marriages of three of George and Alice Mansfield's children were connected with their parents' social network (Esmonde, More O'Ferrall and Farrell), other factors influenced the marriages of Margaret, Eustace and Henry. In 1911, Eustace, the eldest son, married Mabel Paget, a Catholic English lady and daughter of a banker, in London.[42] The marriage announcement in the *Leicester Daily* points to what may have been a connection with the Mansfield social network, in that it states that the Forbes family, part of the Mansfield network, were cousins of the bride. It is also notable that this is the first instance in which the French connection, through Alice's family, was evident in any of her children's marriages – specifically, Eustace chose his French cousin Raymond de Mareuil as his best man.[43] Eustace's daughter, Rosalind, George and Alice's granddaughter, married one of the Sweetman family in 1941 and thus the intermarriage pattern among families and kin did continue into the next generation.[44] Margaret Cecile Mansfield (fig. 8), the youngest daughter, was married twice, on both occasions in London, with both husbands Catholic and in the cavalry.[45] While it has not been possible to definitively know how Margaret met both her husbands, once again, it may be that there is a family connection through her brothers, all three of whom fought in the First World War, or through their school network. Margaret's brother, Henry Marie Lattin Mansfield, was a member of the Royal Horse Artillery

8. A young Margaret Mansfield (source: George Mansfield Photographic Archive, Kildare Local Studies & Archives Collections)

when, in London, he married into a Catholic landed-gentry family, Cronin-Coltsman, that was based in Glenflesk Castle in Co. Kerry, with a holding of 10,316 acres in 1876 (*c.*4,175 hectares).[46] There does not appear to have been any connection between the Mansfield and Cronin-Coltsman families prior to their marriage. It is notable that they also married in London rather than in Ireland. George and Alice's children's marriage choices would thus appear to be consistent with Shanks, who stated that, for landed gentry in Northern Ireland, 'marriage is endogamous in the sense that unions between people of the same social background are encouraged' and that 'marriage with people from other social categories, perceived by them as inferior is, for the gentry, something to be avoided'.[47]

The connection between the Mansfield's choice of education for their children and their social network, as well as the influence that decision had on their marriage choices, are worth consideration. Despite their heritage and connection with France, and their support for equal educational opportunity in Ireland as well as the availability of an elite Catholic boarding school at their doorstep – Clongowes Wood College, established in 1812 and seen as the Eton of Ireland, was only 14km from Morristown Lattin – George and Alice followed the Mansfield family tradition and sent their children to elite Catholic schools in England.[48] In quoting Andrews, Senia Pašeta states that 'those at the "top of the Catholic heap" … sent their sons to schools such as Ampleforth, Stonyhurst or Downside'.[49] Eustace and Henry, like their father George, were educated at Stonyhurst from an early age while Tirso was sent to Downside College in Bath.[50] In addition to being the de facto Jesuit headquarters in England for the majority of the nineteenth century, Stonyhurst, a prestigious and socially exclusive institution, was considered to be one of the top Catholic schools in England. O'Neill suggests that a 'Stonyhurst education … could go a long way in Ireland'; it was a school where many of the boys were from landowner families, with 24 per cent of them expected to inherit landholdings of over 750 acres.[51] In this context, O'Neill states that the 'insularity of the Irish Catholic elite was apparent' and provides examples of families, like GPL and George Mansfield, for whom 'the pattern of success and access to a high-profile education in England was one often transferred from generation to generation … thereby ensuring the social status of the family'.[52] Similarly, Pašeta states that 'Ireland's Catholic elite tended to favour Jesuit schools for their sons … to make social and professional connections that would benefit them later in life' because 'life at these colleges … promised the professional and social success that the Jesuits endeavoured to cultivate'.[53] It is also worth noting that, according to Rothery, the ideal family was undergoing a change of perception in the mid-nineteenth century, and particularly the perception of masculinity, whereby gentry parents sending their children to public elite schools was reflective of a 'belief in the separation of men from the home … and the importance of homosocial interactions' and a growing consensus among the elite that 'a man's formative years should be spent in the company of other men'.[54] Families such as the Thunders and Sweetmans that made up part of the Mansfield core social network also sent their sons to Stonyhurst, leading to a 'pattern of clustered strategic migration' that was common within their network, underpinned by a concern for their 'local reputation'.[55] O'Neill states that, although this behaviour attracted much criticism in the national press, the Catholic elite felt entitled to invest in 'an expensive and elite education' for their children. They did so expecting a return on their investment, specifically 'a real ... social advantage ... upon their repatriation to Ireland', a 'competitive advantage over those Irish Catholics who had remained at home' and an opportunity to 'compete on an almost equal footing with ... established public schools' in England.[56] From this, it is reasonable to conclude that education for the Mansfield boys in England was a function of their social network in Ireland and a preference for maintaining a certain level of social standing among fellow Catholics, and possibly Protestant landed gentry, in Ireland, rather than benefiting from the cultural or networking opportunity afforded them in France.

O'Neill refers to 'instances of Irish boys marrying the English sisters of their schoolmates'; however, following a review of some of the Stonyhurst College Archives, there is no reference to family names Paget or Cronin-Coltsman and thus it does not appear to have been the case for Eustace or Henry Mansfield.[57] Of particular note also is that none of George and Alice's children took husbands or wives of French nationality despite their mother being French and having spent probably up to one-third of their time in France as children, as detailed below. George also spent much time in France with his family prior to his marriage, and the Mansfield family had a network in France, so he too is likely to have been a Francophile. That said, judging by letters sent to their mother from a young age while at Stonyhurst through to the time of the First World War, their written communication with her was in English, although she may have written to them in French.[58] Thus, it would appear that English was the dominant language within the family, which may be one reason why none of their marriage partners were French.

If the choice of Stonyhurst and Downside was rooted in social advantage and social network, it begs the question as to what effect that education had on the future career choice and network of the Mansfield men. George, as the only son of GPL and Mary Mansfield, like many of the boys who attended Stonyhurst, had inherited the family landed estate. As O'Neill states, the 'system of

local government in Ireland depended on the landlord class for its ...
operation until 1898' and indeed, after 1829, the position of JP 'was
a much-sought-after one' to which Catholics were being appointed
more and more often over their Protestant counterparts. With 'almost
a quarter of the Stonyhurst boys' serving 'in a position of local elite
power', it is not surprising that, in addition to his responsibility for
managing the Mansfield estate, George had a local government career
as DL and JP for many years. The Mansfields were like many an 'old
Catholic family' who 'carried on a tradition of public service, and
were consistently visible'. As will be seen later, this afforded George
an opportunity to create a network from public roles that in turn
influenced and overlapped with the family's social network.[59] As
the nineteenth century advanced into the early twentieth century,
however, local government structures began to change in Ireland.
Referring to the roles of DL and JP, O'Neill states that 'these layers
of local government were centuries out of date'. It is perhaps not
surprising then that, with the exception of Eustace, George and
Alice's sons steered away from these public-service roles. Although
Irish Catholics 'were well provided for in terms of third-level
institutions from which to gain degrees for the professions', most
elite Catholics did not attend university at all and the Mansfield boys
were no exception. O'Neill defines the 'ancient learned professions'
as divinity, law, medicine and military, all representing 'a high-
status professional option for elite families'.[60] With the Stonyhurst
tradition and school network as their impetus, Eustace, Henry and
Tirso headed for distinguished military careers, fighting as part of
the British Army in India and later as part of the First World War
in France and Flanders. For Stonyhurst, 'thirty-six per cent of those
whose occupations are known were involved in some capacity in
active service' and thirty-four per cent for Downshire.[61] Eustace
served as a captain with the 3rd Royal Dublin Fusiliers, while Henry,
the second-eldest son, flew with the RAF and was awarded an OBE
in 1918 for his military services (fig. 9).[62]

In summary, the education choices made by George and Alice
strengthened both their and their sons' network and social standing
in Ireland, which was apparently seen as a higher priority than
their maternal connection to, and network in, France. The choice
of school and resulting networks, however, do not appear to have

9. Henry Lattin Mansfield (on right), awarded OBE in 1918 for military service
(source: Stonyhurst War Record (1927))

influenced their marriage choices. The choice of school did lead to a
military career that also improved their social standing and possibly
broadened their social network. Notwithstanding the fact that the
early twentieth century was a time of war during which young men
all over Europe were conscripted or signed up voluntarily for the
army, the choice of George Mansfield's sons fits within the expected
norm for elites, both in Ireland and in France, where Alice's brothers
also embarked on military careers.

To conclude, the Mansfield family were without question of
landed-gentry class and had a strong Catholic identity that stood
to them through centuries of oppression, a reality that will be
substantiated later when looking at their networks in Ireland. For
the Mansfields, marrying within their religion was ultimately more
important than within their class. For class and religion reasons, it was
not unusual to marry into local families that were known to them,
that were trusted, and that in many cases were cousins or other kin.
This marriage pattern may have been driven by a strategy that was
within the norm for their class, that is, to protect their family estate
and associated lands from one generation to another. It would appear

also that they were good landlords who integrated well into the local community, a behaviour that would have made it easier for them to keep the estate intact through difficult times. Finally, for a bi-national family, George and Alice's children's marriages were influenced more by their Irish connections than by their French ones.

2. Catholic elite networks in Ireland through the lens of George and Alice Mansfield

While in Ireland, the Mansfield family resided for most of the time in their big house, Morristown Lattin in Co. Kildare. Although Alice's diary entries are sometimes sporadic, they do provide an entirely adequate representation of where the family spent their time in Ireland for the ten years under review. The map in figure 10 shows Morristown Lattin and the principal locations visited throughout Ireland during that period, based upon an analysis of data extracted from the diary transcriptions.

In her diary from 1877 to 1887, Alice mentions 116 different people and families in Ireland. Appendix 5 shows the names and frequency of mention of these families within her diary. The majority are mentioned once or twice in the space of ten years and thus, while they formed part of the Mansfield network, they cannot be considered as their core network in Ireland. This analysis focuses on that core network, those families and individuals that she mentions four times or more. From a class perspective, the Mansfields' Irish social network was, in the majority, made up of gentry, with some titled, military and religious people. Many of them shared public roles with George, either as JP, DL or leading members of the County Kildare Archaeological Society, of which George was president in 1926.[1] In general, the social network in Ireland came from connections and relationships made in various ways, which for the purposes of this work are classified as family, public, church, CKAS, hunting and racing. The core network is made up of nineteen families as shown in figure 11.

Further details for that core network are shown in table 1. Religion was determined from primary sources that included civil, church and census records, newspapers and peerage publications. The column in

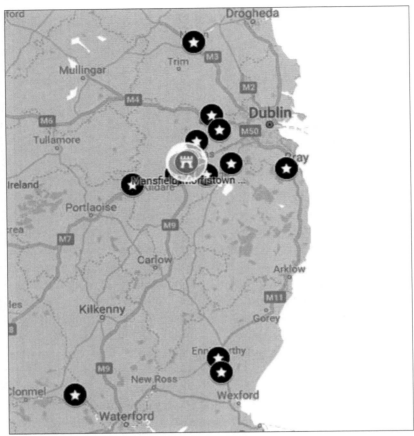

10. Geographic spread of the Mansfield network in Ireland, 1879–89
(source: NLI, Mansfield Papers, MS 38, 423/1)

the table entitled Social Network Nexus is defined as the activity, organization or means through which they met these families or people. These nexuses were identified by triangulating Alice's diary with newspapers and society records. A nexus of church indicates that the connection was made through activities associated with the Catholic Church. From this, it is also possible to see that there were multiple different, often interlocking, nexus for their social network during the ten-year period. The column entitled Location represents the geographical location where the family in question was resident in Ireland, as listed in land records, civil records, newspapers or census

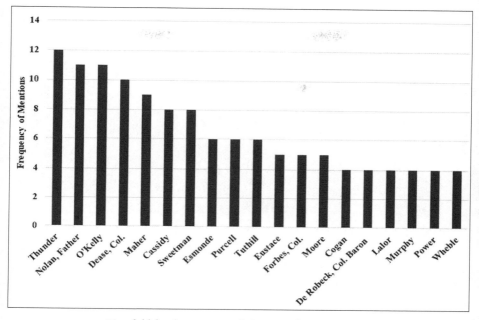

11. Mansfield family core network (source: Alice Mansfield Diary
(NLI, Mansfield Papers, MS 38, 423/1))

Table 1. Mansfield core social network by Frequency of Mention, Nexus, Location, Religion and Class

Family Name	Frequency of Mention	Social Network Nexus	Location	Religion	Class
Thunder	12	Family	Navan, Newbridge, Enniscorthy	Catholic	Gentry
Nolan, Father	11	Church	Dominicans, Newbridge	Catholic	Religious
O'Kelly	11	Family, Hunting	Barretstown	Catholic	Gentry
Dease, Col.	10	CKAS, Public	Celbridge Abbey, Celbridge	Catholic	Gentry
Maher	9	Family, Racing	Ballinkeele House, Enniscorthy, Co. Wexford	Catholic	Gentry
Cassidy	8	Hunting, Racing	Monasterevan	Catholic	Gentry
Sweetman	8	Family	Longtown, Clane, Co. Kildare; Fitzwilliam Square, Dublin	Catholic	Gentry
Esmonde	6	Family (O'Kelly)	Glenbrook House, Enniskerry	Catholic	Gentry
Purcell	6	Hunting	Halverstown, Co. Kildare	Catholic	Gentry
Tuthill	6	Hunting	Moyglare, Co. Meath	Protestant	Gentry
Eustace	5	Family	Yeomanstown, Co. Kildare	Catholic	Gentry
Forbes, Col.	5	Public, Hunting		Protestant	Gentry
Moore	5	Public, Hunting	Killashee House, Naas	Protestant	Gentry
Cogan	4	CKAS, Public	Tinode, Co. Wicklow	Catholic	Gentry
De Robeck, Col. Baron	4	CKAS, Public, Racing, Hunting	Gowran Grange, Naas	Protestant	Gentry
Lalor	4	Racing	Cregg, Co. Tipperary	Catholic	Gentry
Murphy	4	n/a	n/a	Catholic	Gentry
Power	4	Hunting	Edermine, Co. Wexford	Catholic	Gentry
Wheble	4	Hunting; Church	Monasterevan	Catholic	Merchant

(sources: *Burke's landed gentry of Ireland* (1912); *Burke's peerage* (1980); newspapers; GRO
Dublin; Alice Mansfield Diary (NLI, Mansfield Papers, MS 38, 423/1); Journal of CKAS;
Return of owners (1876); Costello, *A class apart* (2005))

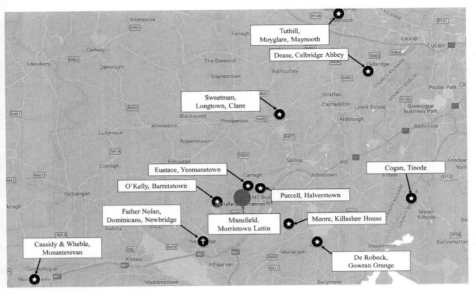

12. Family locations for Mansfield core network
(source: Alice Mansfield Diary (NLI, Mansfield Papers, MS 38, 423/1))

records. The column entitled Class has been determined through peerage records, land records or newspaper descriptions. In this instance, those families classified as gentry are landed gentry listed in land records, those families classified as religious are clerics and those classified as merchant are families that are recorded, typically in newspaper articles, as having built successful businesses.

From a geographical perspective, George and Alice's core network was, not surprisingly, largely in proximity to their home in Morristown Lattin, as can be seen in the map in figure 12. It shows that 75 per cent of the families were within a 20km radius of Morristown Lattin, with the exceptions being five families: Thunder, Esmonde, Maher, Power and Lalor. It is important to note that the family they most frequented, Thunder, was based across multiple locations and, while it is not represented in figure 12, it is represented by the Navan clan in the map in figure 10.

As shown in chapter 1, the Mansfield family would appear to have always been committed Catholics for generations, having remained so through much adversity. For the ten-year period under consideration, their core network was eighty per cent Catholic, as shown in table 1, with Father Nolan, their local curate, the second-most mentioned connection. From his diary entries prior to marrying Alice, it is clear that George Mansfield was a regular church-goer and a committed Catholic, as were previous generations of his family. His father, GPL, is noted as having 'welcomed the Holy Family Sisters when they came to Newbridge ... in 1875 ... to open a convent and school' and GPL 'had provided the site for the parish church and parochial house in the 1840s', the same site on which 'the convent was built'.[2] Indeed, in a letter George wrote to his father from Pau in France on 2 April 1872, he states 'I am quite willing to join you in promising to the bishop a lease forever, at a nominal rent, of the ground the Newbridge convent is to be built on'.[3] A *Leinster Leader* report from January 1890 that lists all of the parishioners who donated to a fund for completion of the Dominican church tower in Newbridge shows George and his father, sister and other family members at the top of the list, and George also as a committee member.[4]

Nevertheless, they also mixed in Protestant circles and the Tuthill family is an example of Protestant landed gentry with whom George and Alice socialized on several occasions both in Ireland and in France. In Ireland, they socialized with Captain William Tuthill and his family, whose big house was at Moyglare in Co. Kildare, and who owned more than one thousand acres in Co. Limerick in 1876.[5] The family of the 4th baron de Robeck were also Protestant landed gentry and were proprietors of Gowran Grange estate in Co. Kildare, which in 1876 consisted of 1,838 acres.[6] Socializing with Protestant elites like the de Robeck and Tuthill families through leisure activities such as the Kildare Hunt was not entirely unusual for Catholic landowners, and a regular occurrence for George Mansfield and his uncles. Both families, part of the Mansfield core social network, also spent time together outside of hunting; for example, in August 1886 Alice noted that they attended both a 'large party' hosted by Baron de Robeck and an evening with the Tuthills in Moyglare.[7] The Mansfield family were also guests at the marriage of Emily, the daughter of Baron de Robeck, an occasion that Alice noted in April 1878. She also noted the death of both Captain Tuthill in 1885 and his wife in 1887.[8]

George travelled to Dublin on 26 April 1878 for a meeting of those in favour of Catholic education and in attendance were parliamentarians, notables and clergy such as the lord mayor, Revd

Dr McGettigan, Hon. W.H.F. Cogan MP and Col. Colthurst, the latter two being part of the Mansfield social network. George was one of the speakers at that meeting; Alice noted in a diary entry that she also attended the meeting and that he had made a good speech.[9] What is clear is that George defended the principle of equal educational opportunity for Catholics in Ireland yet was capable of mixing with ease in either Catholic or Protestant circles and four Protestant families became part of the core network from his public and leisure engagements.[10] This is an example of landed gentry rising above the religious differences that might have divided families of a different class, an arrangement that is likely to have been mutually beneficial.

Of all of the families mentioned in Alice's diary during the ten-year period, eight were related through marriage to the Mansfield family, six of which were in the core network of nineteen families. Making an assumption that the number of mentions is a proxy for time spent with that family, it is possible to state that kin constituted 40 per cent of the Mansfield core social network. It is entirely reasonable to assume that this is typical of landed gentry but may have been lower than normal given the fact that Alice came to Ireland only after her marriage to George, and that family in Ireland was tied exclusively to George's branch. Based on a study of the 1851 and 1881 census returns for 154 households in three counties in England, Rothery advances that 'kin relations were ... central to everyday country-house life' and that 'cousins of a more distant sort were present but in far smaller numbers'.[11] It would appear that Rothery's hypothesis holds true for the Mansfield family, which, as previously mentioned, had three generations living together in Morristown Lattin. The cousin kin connection is also apparent through a Miss Emma Eustace who appears to have lived in the house and is mentioned five times by Alice in the decade, and is often with George and Alice when frequenting their social network.[12]

The Thunder, O'Kelly and Maher families, the three most frequently mentioned in Alice's diary, are all George's kin. As seen in figure 7, the Thunders intermarried with the Mansfields when Eliza, George's aunt, married George Thunder and, as such, they were paternal kin. George and Eliza Thunder lived in Kingstown Lodge, Navan, Co. Meath, and owned 206 acres in 1876.[13] From Alice's diary entries, it appears that George and Alice spent time with different branches of the family, in Newbridge, Navan and Enniscorthy, and that George and Eliza had at least three children, all of whom would have been George Mansfield's first cousins. On Monday 15 October 1877 Alice noted lunch with Mrs Boylan at her home in Bellewstown, Co. Meath, and the Thunder family were also in attendance. The Boylan family were Catholic landed gentry living at Hilltown House, where they owned 2,914 acres in 1876.[14] While they were a part of the Mansfield social network, this was the only visit noted by Alice during the ten-year period. One month later, Alice made a note in her diary of the death of George Thunder at his home and, three days later, of her husband, also George, attending George Thunder's funeral with his father GPL and uncles Edmund and Dick. Almost three months later, 'Aunt' Eliza visited Morristown Lattin with two of her children and stayed for two weeks. Five days after that, another diary entry mentioned that Eliza Thunder had died.[15] Alice's diary entry for St Stephen's Day 1879 stated that she spent the day at the Christmas tree in neighbouring Barretstown with her husband, George, their first child, Mary, the O'Kelly family and the family of Patrick Thunder, a nephew of George Thunder.[16] Alice's diary entries also mentioned health-related news of the Thunder family – in 1878, Marianne Thunder gave birth to a daughter who died after twenty-one days, in 1882 Edmund Thunder had typhoid fever, while in 1885 the same Edmund fell from a bus and broke his arm.[17] Two months later, in May 1885, Alice wrote that Edmund and family were moving to Newbridge to establish a medical practice.[18] On a number of occasions, Alice noted trips to Dublin for lunch or a show with George's Thunder cousins and such social occasions also often involved the Esmonde and Sweetman families, both Catholic landed gentry and both part of the core network. Finally, when her young son Bertrand was suffering from meningitis in April 1887, Alice wrote that she called for Dr Edmund Thunder to replace the family doctor, Dr Faulkner, who, for her, had not looked after Bertrand very well.[19]

The O'Kelly family feature almost as much as the Thunders in Alice's diary, with eleven mentions. George's maternal grandparents were George and Maria Bourke O'Kelly (see figure 7) and thus their grandchildren were George's first cousins and maternal kin. As noted in chapter 1, the Mansfield estate was adjacent to the O'Kelly Barretstown estate, of which the Mansfield family were trustees for two generations; GPL from 1885, in partnership with Arundell de Pentheny O'Kelly and his nephew Mathias Maher, and subsequently George Mansfield, in partnership with George Maher and Francis Thunder. As might be expected, all trustees were related through intermarriage. On numerous occasions, Alice and George socialized with the O'Kelly family, particularly with cousins Marguerite and Johnny O'Kelly; for example, a dinner in January 1878.[20] Alice also noted the guests attending the christening lunches that she hosted in 1878 for Mary and in 1879 for Eustace and on both occasions several members of the O'Kelly family were in attendance.[21] The aforementioned St Stephen's Day 1879 family gathering in Barretstown was hosted by the O'Kelly family. Alice noted that same year, in September, that they had played tennis together with the O'Kellys and others. In February 1882 while the Mansfields were in transit from France to Ireland, they met Blanche O'Kelly, one of George's grandaunts, while staying in London's Euston Hotel.[22]

Louisa Catherine Bourke O'Kelly, a sister of George's mother, married John Maher and their children were also George's first cousins and maternal kin. The Maher family were Catholic landed gentry and their estate centred on Ballinkeele House (fig. 13), near Enniscorthy, Co. Wexford, where it extended to 4,950 acres in 1876.[23] Alice mentioned the Maher family nine times in her diary over the ten-year period. The first mention is October 1877, shortly after her arrival in Ireland, when, with George, they travelled to Ballinkeele to visit Mr and Mrs Maher and George's cousins, and stayed for eight days. During that time, they had lunch with another Catholic landed gentry family, the Cliffes, in their home, Bellevue House, Co. Wexford, then dinner with the Walkers and Colonel Alcock, and returned to have tea with the Walkers a couple of days later.[24] They also visited in Edermine, Co. Wexford, the Powers, another Catholic landed-gentry family that were part of their core network during the ten-year period.

George and Alice's first child, Mary, was born in July 1878 and Alice's diary entry on the day of Mary's christening mentioned Mrs Maher as the godmother. Of the Maher cousins, Alice mentioned Louisa and Matty on a number of occasions, attending Punchestown and Curragh horse racing in 1883 and 1885 respectively, with Louisa and Matty having spent a few days at Morristown Lattin in June

13. Ballinkeele House, Enniscorthy, Co. Wexford
(source: Ballinkeele House (www.ballinkeele.ie), 16 July 2019)

1886. Working together as trustees of the O'Kelly estate, Matty and GPL did not always agree on how tenant relations should be handled during times of rent arrears in Clongorey and the Plan of Campaign.[25] Indeed, according to Ryan, GPL, 'an amicable man, was agreeable in the early stages to granting rent reductions' whereas 'as time went by Maher became aggressive towards the tenants' and GPL 'came under pressure from … Maher', a result of which was the resignation of GPL's as a trustee of the estate. It is thus remarkable and very telling of the importance of kin within their network that such good relations persisted between the next generation of Maher and Mansfield families, despite the tensions that would have existed between GPL and Matty Maher.[26]

Rothery highlights what he sees as a limitation in history-of-family scholarship. He maintains that, due to the system of primogeniture, a holistic view has not been taken of gentry kin networks. He argues that gentry families socialized bilaterally, that is, with both paternal and maternal kin. This bilateral nature of their kinship was key to their identity and sociability and 'marital kin were not merely tolerated or entertained but played a functional role in landed-gentry life … psychological support … maintaining wealth, careers and reputations'.[27] The above analysis of the Mansfield core network supports Rothery's hypothesis in a number of ways. As noted, the Maher and O'Kelly families were George's maternal kin, while the Thunder family were paternal kin. George's maternal kin in general appear to have played a role in George and Alice's social network that was at least as significant as paternal kin. From Alice's diary, it would appear that the events and occasions undertaken with the Thunders as paternal kin differed little from those undertaken with the O'Kelly and Maher families – activities such as visits to Dublin, visits to each other during the Christmas period and entertainment in Morristown Lattin. The influence of maternal kin for their children, that is, Alice's family, is discussed in the following chapter, which considers networks based in France. The distance from maternal kin led to a rather unique situation, with the children's paternal kin, George's cousins and their children, playing the biggest role when in Ireland.

Throughout the eighteenth and nineteenth centuries, the landlord was seen as the 'arbiter of power and privilege' within a system in which the 'law of the land was mediated through the estate's representatives', where 'magistrates and justices of the peace were usually landowners' and where 'political representation ... was seen as the entitlement of the landowning classes'.[28] Although the landed-gentry classes were dominated by Protestants, Catholic landed gentry also served in public-administration roles, with the Mansfield family doing so for Co. Kildare for at least four generations. George's grandfather, Alexander Mansfield, was a magistrate for the county in 1818 while his father, GPL, was JP from 1848, DL in 1874 and high sheriff in 1854. George himself was appointed JP in 1866 and DL for the county in 1894 and his eldest son, Eustace, followed in his footsteps as JP in 1908.[29] It is thus not surprising that the Mansfield family's social network was influenced by these public roles. On 11 July 1883 the Kildare county grand jury met in the crown court in Naas for the assizes. The high sheriff of the county, Thomas J. de Burgh, along with his deputy, Henry A. Lee, proceeded to have twenty-three grand jurors sworn into office.[30] As well as George, this included eleven people who were part of his social network, all among the leading landowners of the county. As well as their official function, which was to hear criminal and civil law cases, the

> Twice-yearly assizes ... were great social occasions in Naas, as some of the wealthiest men in the county arrived for meetings that could last two or even three days. Money was spent, politics discussed, business contacts made and renewed, and a lively atmosphere prevailed.[31]

Clearly, this was a network that transgressed its public function and overlapped with the social network of many of the jurors.

As Rachel Murphy states, 'boundaries between work and leisure remained more blurred for the ... elite' in comparison to 'working and middle classes' who 'had a fixed daily pattern ... between work and spare time' and indeed the Mansfield social network had a notable overlap with the network created by their public administration and related roles.[32] Four of the twenty-three jurors, De Robeck, Sweetman, Cogan and Moore, were part of their core social network. The Sweetman family were also related to the Mansfield family through marriage and Alice noted having dinner in August 1884 and tea in October the same year at the Sweetmans' home in FitzWilliam Square, Dublin.[33] Many of the grand jurors were Protestant, and many of the families that George and Alice Mansfield met in both a public and a private capacity were Protestant landed gentry. Thus, to hold public roles of power, it was a requirement for Catholics to be able to work together with Protestants, with class as their common ground, and they would appear to have been seen as equals. Another example of the Mansfield core social network overlapping with George's public connections is the County Kildare Archaeological Society, the inaugural meeting of which George attended in May 1891 at the residence of the earl of Mayo. Again, many of the same landed-gentry names appear among the twenty-seven people in attendance, of which six were referenced in Alice's diary. George was elected as part of the first council on that occasion, where Protestants and Catholics were present, resulting in a council that was made up of both religions – once again an example in which class prevailed over religion.[34]

From 1877 to 1887, the leisure activities that Alice wrote of in her diary are almost exclusively those undertaken by George and it is the people and families whom they met through the latter's activities that formed part of their Irish social network. Like many elite and landed gentry families of the time, there appears, from Alice's diary, to have been much time in George's life for leisure. Racing, hunting, tennis and cricket were his primary leisure activities in Ireland and these pursuits are mentioned throughout the diary; half of the families in the core social network shared one of these activities. The social network that George had constructed for himself and his family from these activities appears to have started prior to his marriage to Alice, as his diary entries from 1873 spoke almost exclusively of such activities, in particular of hunting.[35] Hunting was a favourite activity for landed gentry and the upper classes in nineteenth-century Ireland and, in speaking of Co. Westmeath, Tom Hunt maintains that typical hunting social structure 'was dominated by members of the local aristocracy and gentry, supplemented by officers from ... the military barracks'.[36] Co. Kildare had a particularly active scene as it had benefited from 'a government decision in 1810 to build a barracks for 300 men at Naas' and later from the 'construction of a barracks for almost one thousand men and 980 horses close to the River Liffey at Newbridge'. Con Costello notes that 'both the gentry and the military had a common interest in the horse' and 'meets of the Kildare Hunt Club' and 'Punchestown Races from 1850, were major sporting and social occasions'.[37] Morristown Lattin was approximately 6km from that barracks in Newbridge and the Mansfield family, for several generations, was involved with the hunting fraternity in Co. Kildare.[38] It is also worth noting that the majority of the results from an internet search of the *Leinster Express* and *Leinster Leader* newspapers from 1877 to 1887, with George Mansfield as a key search phrase, relate to either hunting with the Kildare Harriers or participation in tennis tournaments.[39]

Murphy advances the hypothesis that, while such activities might be 'considered "leisure"' pursuits, 'they frequently had an underlying purpose' such as 'political networking'.[40] Indeed, within the Mansfield core social network, of the eleven families involved with George's leisure activities, at least three overlap with his public activities. As Costello states in speaking of the military, 'sometimes the officers entertained members of the Kildare hunt in barracks' and in 1865 they 'gave a breakfast to several gentlemen ... in Newbridge barracks', including the 'marquis of Drogheda, the baron de Robeck, H.G. O'Kelly and E.A. Mansfield'.[41] The first three of these families formed part of the Mansfield core social network and E.A. Mansfield was George's uncle. It is also to be noted that De Robeck shared public life and racing activities with George, thus validating Murphy's hypothesis. In November 1879, Alice wrote in her diary that she was having contractions all day and gave birth to Eustace Lattin, their eldest son, at twenty minutes to eight in the evening. She finished

THE MASTERSHIP OF THE KILDARE HOUNDS.

On Monday last an important meeting of the members of the Kildare Hunt was held at Wynne's Royal Hotel, to report as to the best arrangements for the future hunting of the county, as the committee appointed at last meeting have not yet found a master to succeed Mr Mansfield; a scheme for the separation of the county from the management of the hounds; and other matters of importance were brought under consideration of the meeting.

The Marquis of Drogheda in the chair.

Other members present—The Earl of Clonmell, Lord Maurice Fitzgerald, Hon. T. O. Scott, Hon. Edward Lawless, Mr Richard Moore, Mr G. P. Lattin Mansfield, Captain E. A. Mansfield, Mr Francis Freeman, Mr James Whitelaw, Mr Horace Rochfort, Mr Ambrose More O'Ferrall, Mr Percy La Touche, Mr Wm. Blacker, Mr Robert Kennedy, Captain R. W. Mansfield, Mr Jacob Sherrard, Mr David Mahony, Hon. Secretary; and Captain W. Tuthill.

14. GPL Mansfield and brothers in the Kildare Hunt
(source: *Leinster Express*, 27 Jan. 1877)

that entry by saying that George had been hunting with the Carragh Harriers, which points to the importance of hunting as an activity to George, whether for leisure or for political purposes, or both, in addition to what it could suggest regarding the relative importance of his family.[42]

Hunting had a social side to it too and the 'hunting season always closed with the Kildare Hunt Ball, held in the Naas Town Hall from 1860 onwards', and this provided an opportunity for Alice and other wives to strengthen the social network created by their husband's hunting activities.[43] The *Leinster Express* reported on the ball in 1879, describing a grandiose event as well as the music played on that occasion. Listed among those present were George, Alice and George's sister, Maude.[44] Of that list, six families formed part of the Mansfield core social network. While it is perhaps not unusual to see that the Mansfield family, as landed gentry, engaged in hunting, what can be added is that it transgressed religious boundaries by comprising Catholic and Protestant landed gentry. One example of that transgression can be seen from Mansfield attendance at the funeral on 15 December 1884 of Protestant Edith Cane, a young lady who had died as part of a hunting accident and had been helped by 'Uncle Edmund' following the accident.[45] This is another example of where, for the Mansfield social network, class was more important than religion.

According to Hunt, 'cricket, polo and tennis ... were closely associated with members of the hunting community; the latter two ... the preserve of landed society'.[46] During the nineteenth century, the sport of tennis was considered ideal for landed gentry, with their large lawns and demesnes, which provided them with an opportunity to extend social activities beyond the big house. It differed from other sports in that the guests 'were active participants' and the occasion allowed for 'social networking' and a chance to engage in 'courtship ritual'.[47] In Ireland it started to move out of the landed-gentry private demesnes late in the century with 'the formation of "publicly accessible" clubs' such as the FitzWilliam Lawn Tennis Club in 1877, catering for 'those involved in local administration, members of the local landed gentry, the higher-status professionals and officers'. Like hunting, it was 'closely associated with the Protestant church', a typical example being the Mullingar club, which had a '91 per cent Protestant membership'.[48] As one of Co. Kildare's elite society, George Mansfield showed a keen interest in tennis, both as a player and as an organizer. He was a committee member for the Co. Kildare Club Lawn Tennis Tournament in 1881. Of the nine-person committee at the time, four men and their families were part of the Mansfield network, and the majority were Protestants.[49] Alice wrote in her diary of an 1879 summer holiday, where they stayed at the Breslin Hotel in Bray, Co. Wicklow, for about three weeks and during which George appears to have played tennis almost every second day. He was typically playing on private courts of landed gentry families like the Esmondes in Enniskerry, Co. Wicklow, who were part of their core network and the Farrells of Thornhill, Enniskerry, who hosted a lawn tennis party on 15 August 1879.[50] While both of these families were Catholic, it is reasonable to state that tennis was another activity in which, for the Mansfield family social network, class appears to have been more important to the relationships than religion, particularly when there was an overlap with George's public network.[51]

In summary, the Mansfield family were committed Catholics and, while their Irish social network was largely Catholic gentry, it was not exclusively so. It was fundamentally local and the most active part of the network were kin, George's maternal cousins in particular. Thus, maternal kin were certainly more active than paternal kin. Beyond kin, the social network was made up largely of connections from families associated with George's public administration and leisure activities, where class tended to prevail over religion. The Mansfield family microstudy shows that, during the nineteenth century, public administration responsibilities were given to Catholics as much as to Protestants and that they had a considerable impact on their social network. The connections made from public administration activities were built up over many generations, as were those made from leisure activities such as hunting. The Mansfield family, as landed elite, is also an example of a blurring in the boundaries between leisure activities and public activities, with the former strengthening the connections made from the latter and thus their social network. Finally, it can be concluded that the most important influence on the family social network while in Ireland was George, through his maternal kin and his leisure and public activities.

3. The impact of adding a bi-national dimension to an Irish Catholic elite network

Although born in New York of an American mother, Alice lived in Paris with her father and brother Amedée following her parents' separation, when she was in her early twenties or possibly earlier.[1] From reviewing correspondence between Alice and her mother between 1861 and 1874, it appears that they conversed in French up to 1868 and in English thereafter, the change possibly occurring around the time of her parents' separation.[2] As with her diary, the correspondence Alice received between 1880 and 1916 from friends and family outside Ireland was always written in French.[3] Letters from her children were in English.[4] It is thus probable that Alice was perfectly bilingual but that her preferred language was French. Alice's role in building the Mansfield social network in Ireland was almost certainly compromised by virtue of her *différence* as a Parisian lady who had just recently integrated into society in Ireland but most probably not because of a lack of ability to speak English. With the De Férussac family living in France, she nevertheless had less opportunity to entertain within her kin-group than would have been the case for Irish-born elite women. This is likely to have meant that there was more emphasis on cultivating relations with her family-in-law as part of the Mansfield social network, on her children or on supporting her husband in the activities he undertook as part of that network, rather than in creating her own network.

Alice's diary during the ten-year period 1877–87 shows that the Mansfield family certainly were hosted more often than they entertained in Morristown Lattin. Indeed, she appears to have hosted visitors fewer than a dozen times during that period, two of which were modest parties of about ten to fifteen people to celebrate the christening of her children while the other occasions were visiting family members: the Thunders for two weeks in 1878, George's granduncle and family for fifteen days in 1885 and again in 1886, Matthias Maher for three days in 1886 and the Esmondes for eight days for a tennis tournament in 1884.[5] This behaviour is in line with Rothery's findings for the Fergusson-Davie family, English landed gentry who, during the nineteenth and early twentieth centuries, 'played host to a close set of kin rather than more distant relations' and for whom 'kin were far more prominent than other types of visitor', forming the 'predominant fodder for sociability'.[6]

O'Riordan states that, in Ireland, hosting and entertaining were among 'the primary roles as the wife of a prominent gentleman' and that 'for such women, entertaining' was both 'a leisure pursuit' and 'a requirement of their social position'.[7] MacKnight has shown that being 'a good hostess was a serious ambition for upper-class women' in France.[8] Alice Mansfield fulfilled neither of these stereotypes of an elite wife during that period of her life. While in Ireland, Alice appears to have played a discrete supporting role in building the Mansfield social network as opposed to proactively organizing hospitality to 'uphold her husband's position, maintain the family's reputation, further his and the children's interests and demonstrate class solidarity'.[9]

Nevertheless, Alice gradually became more independent, more engaged with her network outside of Ireland, and involved in activities of her own as her children grew older and as she entered the next stage of the family lifecycle. Interpreting correspondence she received between 1880 and 1916 from all over the world, there is evidence that she was making a concerted effort to entertain regularly at Morristown Lattin and to build her own network in Ireland.[10] For example, she is listed in a newspaper article in November 1914 as a member of the Co. Kildare Distress Committee, which was set up to support cases of poverty and deprivation as a result of the First World War, a conflict in which three of her sons were engaged. Several of her fellow committee members were in common with the family social network, notably Lady Mayo, Miss de Robeck and Mrs Cassidy, and, once again, we see the ability to mix with Protestants.[11]

During the ten-year period under consideration, the Mansfield family split their time between Ireland and France, as might be expected for a bi-national family. They did this – and often in

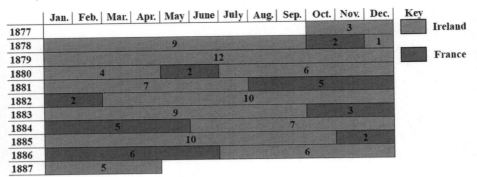

15. Mansfield family location, 1877–87
(source: Alice Mansfield Diary, 1877–87 (NLI, Mansfield Papers, MS 38,423/1))

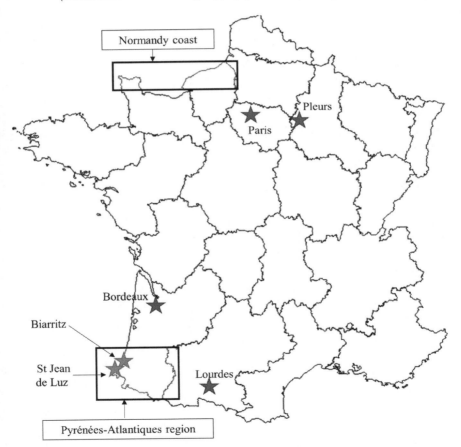

16. Map view of the Mansfield family locations in France, 1877–87
(source: Alice Mansfield Diary, 1877–87 (NLI, Mansfield Papers, MS 38,423/1))

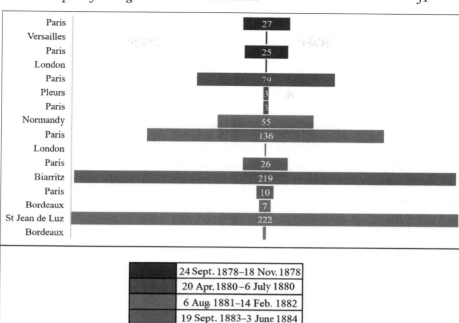

	24 Sept. 1878–18 Nov. 1878
	20 Apr. 1880–6 July 1880
	6 Aug. 1881–14 Feb. 1882
	19 Sept. 1883–3 June 1884
	20 Oct. 1885–9 June 1886

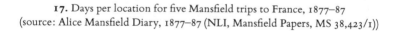

17. Days per location for five Mansfield trips to France, 1877–87
(source: Alice Mansfield Diary, 1877–87 (NLI, Mansfield Papers, MS 38,423/1))

large numbers – despite the challenges associated with travel in the nineteenth century. A typical journey took two or three days and required multiple trains, sea crossings and nights in accommodation in England and either Ireland or France. Impending childbirth did not appear to stop Alice from travelling to France with the family and on one occasion she gave birth in France, to Margaret Cecile, her youngest daughter, in November 1883, only two months after her departure from Morristown Lattin.

While such a lifestyle is a manifestation of their wealth and status, it was also made possible by the ability to depend on their family network, Alice having left France only in 1877 and thus still having connections back in her home country. Figure 15 shows the family location month-to-month from 1877 to 1887.[12] During that time, they spent on average just under four months per year in France and the remainder of their time in Ireland. The only discernible pattern is that from 1881 and every second year thereafter, they spent seven or eight months in France, typically for autumn and winter. In 1879, they did not spend any time there. It is possible that Alice preferred to give birth at home in Ireland, which would have dictated the timing of trips to France, with the previously noted exception.

Between 1877 and 1887, the Mansfield family made five trips to France and an analysis of Alice's diary shows that they split their time during those trips primarily between Paris, where Alice's father and siblings resided, and locations in the Pyrénées-Atlantiques south-west region such as Pau, Biarritz and St Jean de Luz, which were popular nineteenth-century holiday locations for the elite in France (figs 16, 17, 18).[13]

The first two of these trips, in 1878 and 1880, were to Paris and the surrounding area for approximately two months and three months respectively. The third trip, in 1881, was again to Paris for six months, following approximately two months spent along the Normandy coast in the late summer. The fourth and fifth trips were to Biarritz in 1883 and St Jean de Luz in 1885. In 1883, they spent a month in Paris before going to Biarritz, with George going ahead by a week to locate a holiday home in which the family would stay. In 1885, the same pattern occurs, with George going ahead to locate a place to stay, however on that occasion the family transited via Bordeaux rather than Paris. On both occasions, they spent about seven months in the south-west while making numerous excursions to the surrounding areas. Karl Baedeker states that Biarritz was 'specially frequented by the upper classes, by the aristocracy of southern France and by Spaniards in summer, and by the English in winter', which suggests that George and Alice are conforming more to the norms of English and Irish people than the French when in Biarritz.

The time spent by the Mansfield family in France was always for leisure or holiday including visiting family. The network in France would appear to have been just as extensive as in Ireland, with Alice mentioning 108 different families in her diary. Appendix 6 shows the name and frequency of mention of these families. As in Ireland, many of the families are mentioned only once or twice in the space of ten years and thus cannot be considered as their core network in France. The twenty-one families that are mentioned three or more times in Alice's diary, that core network, are represented in figure 19 from which it is possible to see an overlap with their network in Ireland

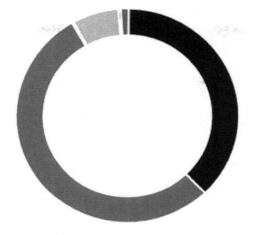

■ Paris ■ Pyrenees-Orientales ■ London ■ Normandy ■ Pleurs ■ Bordeaux

18. Division of time across locations outside Ireland, 1877–87
(source: Alice Mansfield Diary, 1877–87 (NLI, Mansfield Papers, MS 38,423/1))

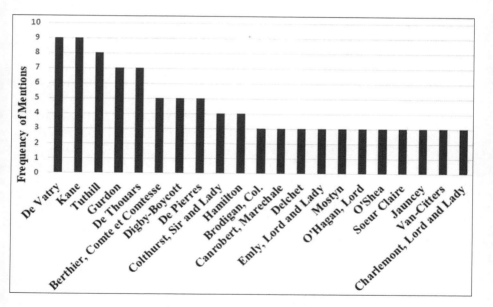

19. Frequency of diary mentions of families while in France
(source: Alice Mansfield Diary, 1877–87 (NLI, Mansfield Papers, MS 38,423/1))

Table 2. French core social network, families mentioned three or more times, 1877–87

Family Name	Frequency of Mention	Social Network Nexus	Location of Mansfields when mentioned	Religion
De Vatry	9	Family	Paris, Biarritz	Catholic
Kane	9	Ireland	St Jean de Luz	Protestant?
Tuthill	8	Ireland	St Jean de Luz	Protestant
Gurdon	7	-	Biarritz	Catholic
De Thouars	7	-	Biarritz	Catholic
Berthier, Comte et Comtesse	5	-	Paris, Biarritz	Catholic
Digby-Boycott	5	Social, Church?	Biarritz, St Jean de Luz	Catholic
De Pierres	5	Family	Ireland, Biarritz	Catholic
Colthurst, Sir and Lady	4	Ireland	St Jean de Luz	Protestant
Hamilton	4	Ireland	Biarritz, St Jean de Luz	Protestant?
Brodigan, Col.	3	Ireland	St Jean de Luz	Catholic
Canrobert, Marechale	3	-	Paris	Catholic
Delchet	3	Hunting	Paris	Catholic
Emly, Lord and Lady	3	Ireland, Hunting	St Jean de Luz	Catholic
Mostyn	3	Ireland	St Jean de Luz	Catholic
O'Hagan, Lord	3	Ireland, Hunting	Biarritz	Catholic
O'Shea	3	Ireland?	Biarritz	Catholic?
Soeur Claire	3	Family, Church	Paris	Catholic
Jauncey	3	Family	St Jean de Luz	Catholic
Van-Citters	3	-	St Jean de Luz	Protestant
Charlemont, Lord and Lady	3	Ireland, Hunting	St Jean de Luz	Protestant

(sources: Alice Mansfield Diary, 1877–87 (NLI, Mansfield Papers, MS 38,423/1); Geneanet; *Burke's landed gentry of Ireland* (1912); *Burke's peerage* (1980); *Debretts illustrated peerage* (1893); newspapers; Crisp, *Visitation of England and Wales*, 17 (1911))

through two families, Tuthills and Colthursts (the Hamilton family in France appear to be a different branch from the one in Ireland). Approximately half of the families were French with the other half either Irish or English. It has not been possible to determine whether the Tuthill and Colthurst families spoke French or had connections with France in any way, although other Irish families in their French network did. From a class perspective, their network in France was in the majority made up of gentry with several titled families, as well as some military. This of course does not take account of the fact that George, Alice and family spent most of their time in France with Alice's kin – her father Baron de Férussac and her sister Henrietta or brothers Amédée and Louis, either in Paris or in the south-west.

An analysis of the French core network is represented in table 2. In this instance, a descriptor of Ireland in the Social Network Nexus column represents a family that is recorded in land records, peerage records or newspapers as based in Ireland without specifying if that is for the majority of the year or not. In the case of several French families, it has not been possible to definitively identify how they came to be part of the network, however it is possible that they were Alice's father's connections as a result of military activities. The Location column differs this time in that it represents the geographic location of the Mansfield family when the networked family was mentioned in Alice's diary, rather than the principal residence of the networked family. This approach was taken because, in many cases, the interaction with the Mansfield family was in the temporary holiday setting of south-west France. For table entries that end with a question mark, it has not been possible to substantiate with a primary or secondary source.

The majority of their French network was Catholic with a few Protestant families, including those that they met with most frequently, such as the Tuthills. Indeed, there are great similarities between the Irish and French core networks in terms of religion and class.

As they were typically on holiday while in France, their network would appear to revolve exclusively around social and leisure activities. George's leisure activities while in Biarritz or St Jean de Luz differed somewhat from in Ireland, with participation in photography, climbing and golf although Alice did note twice in her diary that he went hunting, in 1883 and 1885.[14] In May 1886, Alice recorded that she had been suffering from a fever and George had decided to bring her away for a four-day trip into the Pyrenees. She also noted that they had hired a guide, who carried George's photography equipment, that George was on foot and that she rode on a horse. They finished their trip with a visit to the grotto in Lourdes.[15] This is one of the few occasions during the ten-year period that the couple appear to have shared leisure time together, without their social network, Alice's family or their children. It is also one of the few occasions during that period for which Alice's diary gives a sense of some affection between herself and George.

For their first trip to Biarritz from 1883 to 1884, Alice mentioned that they travelled with three children although there were four children alive at that stage – Mary, Eustace, Henry and Alexander – 5, 4, 2 and 1 years old respectively and Alice gave birth to her fifth

child, Marguerite, a month after their arrival. It is not clear which
child was left in Ireland nor why that would be the case, nor with
whom they would have stayed, other than possibly GPL and his
daughter Maude. Alice's father also travelled with them from Paris,
as did apparently at least two nannies. While there, they were visited
on several occasions by family, notably Alice's brother and George's
uncles, as well as friends. Alice noted several daytrips in her diary
and one multi-day trip into the north of Spain, usually with friends
and family but never with all of the children. On three occasions,
she mentioned the children, once where she took them to a party,
another where she took them to a fair in Bayonne and another time
where, with her father, she took three of the children to Bayonne.[16]
On several occasions, George is noted as heading to different places
seemingly alone. During this stay in Biarritz, Alice made note of
seven occasions when she and George had tea or dinner with other
families from their network, several from their core network such
as De Thouars, Gurdon, Hamilton, Digby-Boycott, O'Hagan and
O'Shea and others outside their core network such as De Lartigues,
De Luppe and Lawless.

For their second trip to the south-west of France, from 1885 to
1886, they travelled with all six children – Mary, Eustace, Henry,
Alexander, Marguerite and Bertrand – and stayed in St Jean de Luz.
Alice's brother Louis and her father stayed with them. During this
trip, their social-network activities revolved around the children. On
St Stephen's Day in 1885, they hosted a children's party and in 1886,
for Alexander's fourth birthday, they also hosted a party.[17] On three
other occasions during their stay Alice noted the children attending
parties hosted by families within their network.[18] While Alice also
attended these parties, it is not clear whether George did. It has
not been possible to identify how all of the host families and those
attending the parties became part of George and Alice's network,
however it is likely that some of them would have been previously
part of Alice's social network or, in the case of the Tuthill family, their
network in Ireland. With children from the Kane, Digby-Boycott
and O'Shea families also attending these parties, it is also possible that
these were part of the Mansfield social network prior to George and
Alice's marriage, given that the Mansfield family spent some time
in the Biarritz area, although it has not been possible to prove this.

While many of the same families from their 1883–4 trip still formed part of their social network in 1885, there were a number of new names, such as the Tuthill family, who, although Protestant, were mentioned more frequently than all but two other families during their five visits to south-western France. Indeed, Alice wrote in her diary of meeting Mrs Tuthill and her four daughters in the railway station prior to their train journey from Bordeaux to St Jean de Luz.[19] As well as the children's parties, they appear to have made more day excursions this time than in 1883–4, and usually with families from their social network that had children. For example, between 28 November and 7 December 1885, they made three daytrips with the Tuthill family.[20] They also hosted a five-day visit from Alice's first cousin, William Jauncey, and his family during May 1885. The visit included a daytrip with the Kane and De Thouars families and their children to a nearby lake.[21]

As previously noted, George and Alice made two trips exclusively to Paris during the ten-year period, one in 1878, for two months approximately, with a three-month-old Mary and her nanny, and another in 1880, for three months approximately, with Mary, her five-month-old brother Eustace and the same nanny. Alice's diary entries for these two trips are sparse, with only six entries for the two-month trip and eight for the three-month trip. Nevertheless, they do show some interesting differences from their network and activities while in the south-west. Considering Paris is a major city, it is not unexpected that, while there, their leisure activities were more focused on culture and the arts. For example, on 4 October 1878, George went to an art exhibition with his brother-in-law Amédée and that same evening they went to an opera as a group of eight family and friends, including Alice's father and sister. Two weeks later, they went to a ball in Versailles, just outside Paris.[22]

In 1880, it would appear that the initial impetus for their trip was the marriage of Alice's sister, Henrietta. During that trip, Alice noted visits to the Conciergerie museum with George and her father, as well as an outing to the opera *Aida* with George and another couple.[23] It is worth noting, for two reasons, that the receptions for Henrietta's wedding were hosted in the residence of Baronne Maria de Vatry – first, because the De Vatry family were the most frequently mentioned during all trips to France in the ten-year period

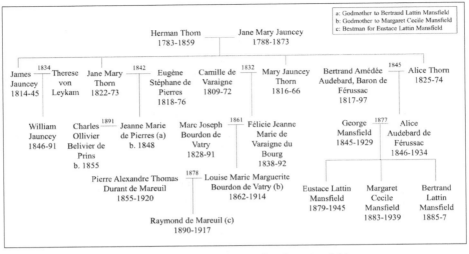

20. Maternal kin connections for Alice Mansfield
(sources: Geneanet.fr; *New York Herald*, 2 Aug. 1859; Cameron Allen, *The history of the American Pro-Cathedral of the Holy Trinity, Paris (1815–1980)* (San Francisco, CA, 2012))

and second they were Alice's first cousins.[24] Offering their residence as the venue for the wedding is evidence of the strong familial ties with the De Vatry family.

Alice's influence on the network appears to have been greatest while in Paris, the only times during the ten-year period when her relationships were the primary source of the family's social network. It is during those trips that the bi-national dimension of the family differentiates the Mansfields and their social networks from the more traditional Irish Catholic elite. That said, Alice's network and relationships appear to be those of the De Férussac family, maternal kin in particular, rather than of Alice herself. The core network in France, shown in table 2, can be categorized into maternal kin like the De Vatry, De Pierres and Jauncey families (figure 20 shows the kin connections), then family connections that appear to emanate from military friends that her father would have had, such as Berthier and Canrobert, and finally families with an Irish or English connection. Alice's social network in France was thus likely to have been bounded by her family connections and her father and husband's social networks.

The influence of Alice's maternal kin on the Mansfield social network while in France is notable, as her mother and father had previously separated and her mother was deceased before her diary was written. Nevertheless, possibly as a result of her father being an only child, Alice maintained strong links with her maternal De Pierres, De Vatry and Jauncey cousins, one of whom was a godmother to her daughter Margaret and another a godmother to her son Bertrand.[25]

The situation whereby the Colthurst and Tuthill families were part of both their Irish and their French networks would no doubt have strengthened their Irish social network and George's public roles in Ireland, with which there was an overlap. Of the other Irish families in France, it is possible, from peerage publications and land surveys, to identify Emly, O'Hagan and Charlemont as titled elite and Mostyn as landed gentry, all of whom appeared to spend a considerable amount of time in Ireland.[26] Lord Emly, William Monsell, was a very well-respected landlord with 2,246 acres in Co. Limerick who is said to have treated his tenants very fairly. He was unusual in that he had converted from the Protestant religion to Catholic in 1850.[27] He married a second time in 1857 to a French lady of noble descent from the Loire Valley.[28] Alice wrote in her diary on New Year's Day 1886 of meeting Lady Emly *dans la rue* in St Jean de Luz, apparently for the first time, and she went to her residence about five weeks later, followed by a lunch several months later with George, and Lord and Lady Emly in the Hotel d'Angleterre.[29] While it is unlikely that Lord or Lady Emly truly first became part of the Mansfield social network as a result of a chance meeting in the street, it is more plausible that Lord Emly had previously known George or GPL in Ireland, through their public roles or through membership of a gentleman's club, or that he had met GPL or George through hunting, an activity in which he also liked to participate.

While in Biarritz in 1884, they also visited Lord and Lady O'Hagan during Christmas and were invited to their residence for dinner less than a month later.[30] Lord O'Hagan was originally from Belfast, resided in Co. Tyrone and became Ireland's first Catholic lord chancellor in 1868.[31] Judging from a report of a meeting held in Dublin to discuss a memorial to Lord O'Hagan, it appears that Lord Emly was a close friend, a fact that underscores how the Irish network transferred to France, a network that George and family were also part of, connections that were likely to have strengthened their Irish network.[32]

Lord and Lady Charlemont were also part of the Mansfield core network in France, while at St Jean de Luz. They were Protestant landowners, with 5,903 acres in 1876 in Co. Tyrone, where Lord Charlemont was lord lieutenant and an MP for Armagh.[33] Lord Charlemont, James Molyneux Caulfield, had married the daughter of a rector from Co. Meath in 1883 and it is this Lady Charlemont that Alice wrote of in her diary in 1885 and 1886, having met for tea on both occasions at Lady Charlemont's residence.[34] Lord Charlemont died in January 1892 in Biarritz and is buried in Armagh, thus it is likely that the Irish families in their French core network exemplified typical behaviour, as Baedeker advanced, by spending much time there during the winter.[35] Here again is an example of where the Mansfield family included Protestants in their core network, showing that class prevailed over religion for their social network outside of kin.

George participated in hunting when in Biarritz, a region that appeared to have an active hunting scene and close ties with Ireland.[36] Two of the families that were part of their broader French social network were involved in hunting, the Knox family and the Labat family, both noted as founding members of the Biarritz fox hunt in 1874.[37] Alice noted that George had dinner in December 1883 with Baronne Pritchard, the daughter of Sir Thomas Knox, just after Alice gave birth.[38] Knox was Irish and Protestant and died in Biarritz.[39] Thus, in Biarritz, through his preferred activities, and his connections from Ireland, George was active in cultivating their social network while Alice did so primarily through her kin network.

In summary, the Mansfield family visited France regularly for extended periods where they also had a social network. That network overlapped somewhat with their social network in Ireland, and exhibited very similar characteristics in terms of class, religion and the mix of kin among other families, with kin being the most active. As with Ireland, it was largely, but not exclusively (fig. 21), Catholic and, once again, class prevailed over religion when it came to leisure activities or public administration contacts from Ireland. The analysis shows that Alice had strong links with her maternal kin in France,

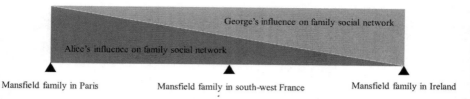

21. Influence of Alice and George on family network is dependent on location

despite her mother being deceased, and kin, coupled with her father's network, constituted her main influence on their social network while in France. That influence was greatest while in Paris.

Thus, the Mansfield family's network while in France was made up of first the Parisian network, led primarily by Alice and family and, second, their network while holidaying in south-west France, composed in relatively equal parts of Alice's kin and of Irish families associated with George's leisure activities and public persona while in Ireland. As represented in figure 21, George's influence on the family social network is greatest while in Ireland, with Alice's greatest while in France, particularly in Paris. Both the Mansfield family and other Irish-based families in their French network exhibited typical behaviour of choosing to visit France during the winter months. The difference in leisure activities between Paris and the south-west is also notable. Finally, when in Ireland, Alice concentrated on playing a discrete supporting role in the context of her husband's social network, while simultaneously cultivating relations with her new family-in-law and focusing on her children.

Conclusion

This study broadens existing scholarship on Catholic landed gentry in Ireland in the late nineteenth and early twentieth centuries through a microstudy of the Franco-Irish Mansfield family in Co. Kildare from 1870 to 1915. It has done so by developing insights into Catholic elite social and marriage networks through that microstudy and by understanding the structure, origins and significance of both Irish and French networks to this bi-national family. Through a thorough analysis of a diary of Alice Mansfield, written between October 1877 and May 1887, and supplemented by research across a wide range of other sources both in Ireland and in France, it has been possible to gain a deeper understanding of this family's social and marriage networks. This is the first time that Alice's diaries, written in French, have been translated and analysed, and as such they provide insights into the activities of this Catholic elite family in late nineteenth-century Ireland.

Through all of the oppression, wars and the Penal-Law period that Catholics endured in Ireland, the Mansfield family remained Catholic. They did so despite the pressure and opportunity to convert to Protestantism. They also held on to, and subsequently grew, their estate in Co. Kildare and maintained excellent landlord–tenant relations during the land wars and agitation of the late nineteenth century.

Analysis of who George and Alice Mansfield socialized with between 1877 and 1887 has shown that their social network was primarily, although not exclusively, Catholic, in both Ireland and France. They also frequented Protestant elite families, however, on a social basis in both countries and typically these Protestants were a part of their social network as a result of George's leisure and public administration activities in Ireland. Indeed, class generally prevailed over religion within their social network for connections other than kin – essentially like-minded people finding each other through common interests and activities. Evidence suggests that their religion was very important to them when it came to marriage. Intermarriage among Catholic elite was a feature and intermarriage among Catholic kin in particular was a characteristic of families in the Mansfield social network for several generations until the mid-nineteenth century.

While kin was the most active part of their social network in Ireland and both maternal and paternal kin were drawn upon, this is different for a bi-national family. As the maternal kin was in France rather than in Ireland, it became part of their social network only when the family were in France, approximately every second year during autumn and winter. The Irish network was constituted primarily of George's contacts through his activities, as well as his family, while the French network presented two different façades, first the Parisian network, led primarily by Alice's contacts and family and, second, their network while holidaying in south-west France, built up in relatively equal parts by Alice's kin and by Irish families associated with George's leisure activities and public persona in Ireland. Maternal kin largely prevailed for both Alice and George, that is, their mother's kin, notwithstanding the fact that both mothers had not been a part of their life for many years prior to their marriage. The bi-national nature of the relationship meant that while, for most of the time, George's network was their network, it broadened that network geographically and strengthened the Irish network.

Analysis of the connection between their social network and their children's education has shown that George and Alice's choice of educational institution for their sons was very much rooted in George's family tradition, that it was considered more important to maintain social status in Ireland than profit from the maternal connection to France, which may have offered an opportunity to further their children's biculturalism or enhance the family's social network. It is most probable that school networks did not influence marriage choices. During the lifecycle stage covered by her diary, Alice had no real network of her own beyond her kin in France and, in particular, she did not have her own local network in Ireland. Contrary to the stereotypical elite woman who proactively entertained in their big house in order to advance their social standing and their husband's standing as a prominent public persona, Alice's approach was that of a discrete supporting partner, focused more on cultivating relations with family-in-law and George's public network.

In doing so, the lack of English-language skills has been discounted, as the family were bilingual to the point that it was unlikely to have negatively impacted their social network in Ireland.

In summary, as the basis for this study, the Mansfield microstudy provides an insight into the social and marriage networks of one Catholic elite family in the late nineteenth and early twentieth centuries and in particular how the bi-nationality of that family influenced those networks and their lifestyle. It also provides an example of what can be termed a self-perpetuating, elite society based on aristocracy rather than meritocracy, prolonged by elite family networks, both Catholic and Protestant, and one that exemplified the same characteristics whether in France or in Ireland. It supports the statement advanced by Dooley that landowners in Ireland shared the same cultural values and social powers irrespective of their religion.[1]

Appendices

APPENDIX I

Sample page from Alice Mansfield's diary while in Ireland, 8 July 1878 to 24 September 1878

APPENDIX 2

Sample transcription and translation of Alice Mansfield's diary page, 8 July 1878 to 24 September 1878

Date	Original French	Translation
8 July 1878	L. 8 - Father Nolan baptise dans la bibliotheque. Mary, Alice, Philomena. Le parrain est le Comte de Férussac et la marraine Mrs Maher (Ballinkeela) ma tante (il fait mes redevailles apres)	Monday 8th - Father Nolan baptises Mary Alice Philomena in the library. The godfather is Count Férussac and the godmother is Mrs Maher (Ballinkeela) my aunt
17 July 1878	mercredi 17 - grand lunch pour feter la naissance de Mary. 20 people les O'Kelly Father Nolan Father Freyne Smith Kinsella. Docteur Falkner. Les Elmar	Wednesday 17th - big lunch to celebrate the birth of Mary. 20 people, the O'Kellys, Father Nolan, Father Freyne Smith Kinsella. Doctor Falkner. The Elmars
19 Aug. 1878	L. 19 août - Mrs Kate Daly entre comme nurse. Mort de M. Beaumon	Monday 19th August - Mrs Kate Daly starts as nurse. Death of Mr Beaumon
28 Aug. 1878	mer. 28 - Lawntennis chez oncle Pen	Wednesday 28th - Lawntennis at Uncle Pen's
6 Sept. 1878	V 6 sept - Docteur Falkner vaccine Mary	Friday 6th Sept. - Doctor Falkner vaccinates Mary
10 Sept. 1878	Mardi 10 - Mon beau frere donne un lawntennis. Temps superbe. 90 personnes. Une trentaine de peches et du raisin du jardin.	Tuesday 10th - My brother-in-law hosts a lawntennis. Superb weather. 90 people. About 30 peaches and grapes from the garden.
24 Sept. 1878	Mardi 24 - Pars pour Paris avec George Mary et nurse. Voyageons en sleeping car. Couchons mercredi a Folkstone. parcourrons toute la ville pour trouver a nous caser arr. J a 6h a Paris. Papa et Nina a la gare.	Tuesday 24th - Leaving for Paris with George, Mary and the nurse. Travelling in sleeping car. Stay in Folkstone on Wednesday. Have to go all around the town to find somewhere to stay. Arrive Thursday in Paris at 6 o'clock. Dad and Nina are at the train station.

(source: Alice Mansfield Diaries, 1877–87 (NLI, Mansfield Papers, MS 38,423/1))

APPENDIX 3

Sample page from Alice Mansfield's diary while in Ireland, 9 January 1884 to 16 February 1884

1884 .

3 Janvier arbre de noel chez Lady O'Hagan .

10 Janvier Amédée mon frère, arrive, vais en voiture avec lui Papa, Aly à la Barre .

12 J Amédée nous quitte pour aller à Toulouse .

17 J soeur Claire va à Lourdes et Papa à Pau voir oncle Henri .

29 Janvier Papa part pour Pleurs grand'mère est très malade .

4 Février Dine avec george chez Lord O'Hagan avec Mrs O'Brien Sir Thomas Knox Bne Pretchard, les Lansitars .

7 Février Uncles Dick et Edmond Mansfield arrivent au Continental H Dick très malade . grand feu d'une écurie vers 10 h du s.

16 Février Marguerite de Natry épouse à St Philippe du roule Jean Monseigneur Langénieux

(source: Alice Mansfield Diaries, 1877–87 (NLI, Mansfield Papers, MS 38,423/1))

APPENDIX 4

Sample transcription and translation of Alice Mansfield's diary page (while in France), 9 January 1884 to 16 February 1884

Date	Original French	Translation
9 Jan. 1884	arbre de Noel chez Lady O'Hagan	Christmas tree at Lady O'Hagan's home
10 Jan. 1884	Amedee, mon frere, arrive, vais en voiture avec lui Papa, Aly a La Barre	Amedee, my brother, has arrived, go by car with him, Dad and Aly [Alexandre] to La Barre
12 Jan. 1884	Amedee nous quitte pour aller a Toulon	Amedee leaves us to go to Toulon
17 Jan. 1884	Soeur Claire va a Lourdes et Papa a Pau voir oncle Henri	Sister Claire goes to Lourdes and Dad goes to Pau to see Uncle Henry
29 Jan. 1884	Papa part pour Pleurs grandmere est tres malade	Dad leaves to go to Pleurs, my grandmother is very ill
4 Feb. 1884	Dine avec George chez Lord O'Hagan avec Mr O'Brien Sir Thomas Knox Baronne Pretchard, les Kansitass	George and I have dinner at Lord O'Hagan's home with Mr O'Brien, Sir Thomas Knox, Baroness Pretchard and the Kansitass
7 Feb. 1884	Uncles Dick et Edmund Mansfield arrivent au Continental. Dick tres malade. Grand feu d'une ecurie vers 10h du soir	Uncles Dick and Edmund Mansfield arrive at the Continental. Dick is very sick. Big fire in a stable around 10 o'clock in the evening
16 Feb. 1884	Marguerite de Vatry epouse a St Philippe du soule par Monseigneur Langenieux, archeveque de Reims, le baron Pierre de Mareuil lieut of 7 reg. de curaissiers temoins Marechal Camrobert Comte de Férussac Generale de Gallifet	Marguerite de Vatry gets married to Baron Pierre de Mareuil, Lieutenant of the 7th Regiment of ??. Ceremony is at St Philippe du Soule and performed by Monseigneur Langenieux, the Archbishop of Reims. Witnesses are Marechal Camrobert, Count Férussac and General de Gallifet

(source: Alice Mansfield Diaries, 1877–87 (NLI, Mansfield Papers, MS 38,423/1))

APPENDIX 5

Frequency of mentions for Mansfield family network in Ireland, 1877–87

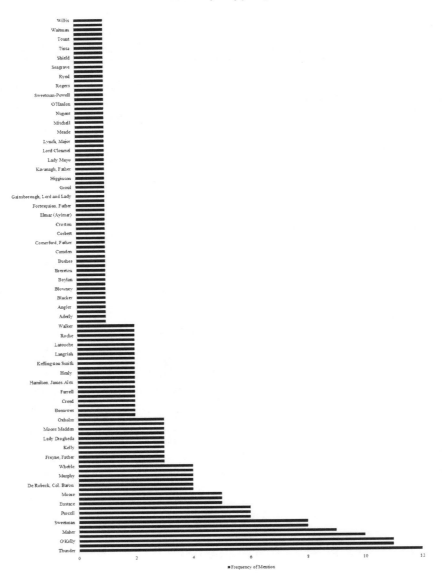

(source: Alice Mansfield Diaries, 1877–87 (NLI, Mansfield Papers, MS 38,423/1))

Frequency of mentions for Mansfield family network in France, 1877–87

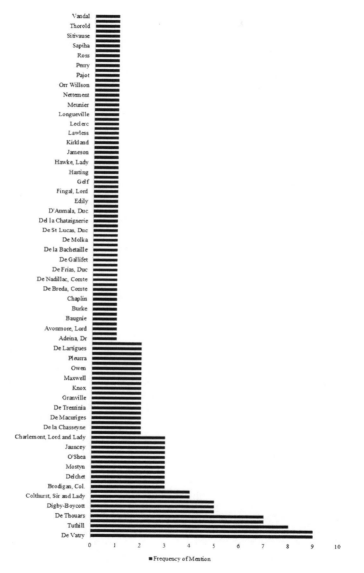

■ Frequency of Mention

(source: Alice Mansfield Diaries, 1877–87 (NLI, Mansfield Papers, MS 38,423/1))

Notes

ABBREVIATIONS

CKAS   County Kildare Archaeological Society
DL   Deputy Lieutenant
GRO   General Register Office, Dublin
JP   Justice of the Peace
LGB   Local Government Board
MP   Member of Parliament
NAI   National Archives of Ireland
NLI   National Library of Ireland
NUI   National University of Ireland
NUIM   National University of Ireland Maynooth
OBE   Officer of the Most Excellent Order of the British Empire
RAF   Royal Air Force
SCA   Stonyhurst College Archives
UCD   University College Dublin
UL   University of Limerick

INTRODUCTION

1 John Tosh, *The pursuit of history* (Harlow, 2010), pp 60–80.
2 Ibid., pp 81–2.
3 Turtle Bunbury and Art Kavanagh, *The landed gentry and aristocracy of Co. Kildare* (Bunclody, 2004); Con Costello, *A class apart: the gentry families of County Kildare* (Dublin, 2005); Terence Dooley, *The big houses and landed estates of Ireland* (Dublin, 2007); Paddy Duffy, 'Colonial spaces and sites of resistance: landed estates in 19th-century Ireland' in L.J. Proudfoot and M.M. Roche (eds), *(Dis)Placing empire* (Aldershot, 2005); Karen Harvey, *The Bellews of Mount Bellew: a Catholic gentry family in eighteenth-century Ireland* (Dublin, 1998); Art Kavanagh and Rory Murphy, *The Wexford gentry* (Wexford, 1994); Emma Lyons, 'Morristown Lattin: a case study of the Lattin and Mansfield families in County Kildare, *c.*1600–1860' (PhD, UCD, 2011); W.A. Vaughan, *Landlords and tenants in mid-Victorian Ireland* (Oxford, 1994).
4 Terence Dooley, *The decline of the big house in Ireland* (Dublin, 2001), p. 11.

5 Ciaran O'Neill, *Catholics of consequence: transnational education, social mobility and the Irish Catholic elite, 1850–1900* (Oxford, 2014).
6 Dooley, *The decline of the big house*; Maeve O'Riordan, 'Leisure with a purpose: women and the entertaining practices of the Irish landed elite, *c.*1860–1914' in Leanne Lane and William Murphy (eds), *Leisure and the Irish in the nineteenth century* (Liverpool, 2016).
7 O'Riordan, 'Leisure with a purpose'; Elizabeth MacKnight, 'Cake and conversation: the women's *jour* in Parisian high society, 1880–1914', *French History*, 19:3 (Oxford, 2005).
8 NLI, Mansfield Papers, Collection list no. 77; LGB, *Return of owners of land of one acre and upwards in the several counties, counties of cities, and counties of towns in Ireland* (1876) (www.failteromhat. com) (13 Apr. 2019); *Griffith's Valuation* (http://askaboutireland.ie/griffith-valuation/) (10 Apr. 2019); Ordnance Survey, Geohive (http://map.geohive.ie/mapviewer.html#) (5 Apr. 2019).
9 Journals of Alice Mansfield, 1877–87 (NLI, Mansfield Papers, MS 38, 423/1).

10 County Kildare Online Electronic History Journal (www.kildare.ie/ehistory) (13 July 2019).

11 Gallica, Bibliothèque Nationale de France (https://gallica.bnf.fr/) (13 July 2019); Les Archives Départementales, Pyrénées Orientales (archives.cd66.fr) (14 July 2019); Paris Archives (archives.paris.fr) (14 July 2019); Geneanet (en.geneanet.org) (14 July 2019).

12 The terms 'kin' and 'kinship' are both used here to refer to a social relationship based on connections from either descent or marriage and are typically used interchangeably throughout with the term 'family'; much of the scholarly work that is referred to uses the kinship terminology rather than 'family'.

13 MacKnight, 'Cake and conversation', p. 342.

1. THE MANSFIELD FAMILY, ESTATE AND MARRIAGE NETWORKS

1 The genealogy of John Mansfield of Ballynamultinagh in the county of Waterford, 1737 (NLI, Mansfield Papers, MS 38, 435/3).

2 Bunbury, *The landed gentry*, p. 145.

3 NLI, Mansfield Papers, Collection list no. 77.

4 Aidan Clarke, 'The colonisation of Ulster and the rebellion of 1641, 1603–60' in T.W. Moody and F.X. Martin (eds), *The course of Irish history* (Cork, 2011), pp 163–75.

5 Charles Chenevix Trench, *Grace's card: Irish Catholic landlords, 1690–1800* (Dublin, 1997), pp 16–17. According to Trench, the 'result of Cromwellian confiscations was that 60 per cent of land owned by Catholics in 1641 was reduced to about 9 per cent by 1660'.

6 Revd Canon Sherlock, 'The Lattin and Mansfield families in County Kildare', *Kildare Archaeological Society Journal*, 3:3 (1900), pp 188–9.

7 Trench, *Grace's card*, p. 58.

8 Harvey, *The Bellews*, p. 14.

9 Ibid., p. 52.

10 Lyons, 'Morristown Lattin', p. 209.

11 Mansfield Pedigree (NLI, Mansfield Papers, MS 38, 434/12); Bunbury and Kavanagh, *Landed gentry*, p. 146.

12 Pedigree of the Lattin family (NLI, Mansfield Papers, MS 38,453/4); John Burke, *History of the commoners of Great Britain and Ireland* (London, 1836), 3, pp 575–6; Bunbury, *Landed gentry,* pp 139–40.

13 Conveyance by Elizabeth and Patrick Lattin to Thomas FitzGerald and James Bulger, 1814 (NLI, Mansfield Papers, MS 38, 266/4).

14 Bunbury, *Landed gentry*, p. 147; O'Kelly Trust (NLI, Mansfield Papers, Collection list 77, p. 156).

15 *Griffith's Valuation* (http://askaboutireland.ie/griffith-valuation/) (10 Mar. 2019).

16 Will of Paulina Mansfield (NAI, Calendar of wills and administrations, principal registry, 1868) (www.willcalendars.nationalarchives.ie) (6 Apr. 2019); LGB, *Return of owners of land of one acre* (1876) (www.failteromhat.com) (14 July 2019).

17 M.B. Ryan, 'The Clongorey evictions' (MA, NUIM, 1999) (http://mural.maynoothuniversity.ie/5108/) (14 Apr. 2019), p. 8.

18 Ryan, 'The Clongorey evictions', pp 21–2.

19 *Leinster Leader*, 12 Jan. 1929.

20 Papers relative to a testimonial from the tenants of the Mansfield estates on the marriage of George Mansfield and Alice d'Audebard de Férussac (NLI, Mansfield Papers, MS 38,421/7).

21 Dooley, *The decline of the big house*, pp 51–2.

22 O'Neill, *Catholics of consequence*, p. 134.

23 Harvey, *The Bellews*, p. 69.

24 Draft will of George Mansfield, 1910 (NLI, Mansfield Papers, MS 38, 388/9).

25 Eustace Mansfield, Morristown Lower, Co. Kildare, Form A, 'Census of Ireland, 1901', NAI (http://census.nationalarchives.ie/reels/nai000912502) (7 Apr. 2019).

26 Dooley, *The decline of the big house*, pp 160–2.

27 Wedding invitation, George Mansfield and Alice De Férussac (NLI, Mansfield Papers, MS 38, 488/4); O'Neill, *Catholics of consequence*, p. 133; Bunbury, *Landed gentry*, p. 149.

28 *Evening Herald*, 14 Mar. 1934.

29 *Burke's Irish family records* (London, 1976), pp 784–5; Sherlock, 'The Lattin and Mansfield families', p. 190; Civil Records (GRO) (www.irishgenealogy.ie) (17 Apr. 2019); George Mansfield, Morristown Lower, Co. Kildare, Form A, 'Census of Ireland, 1911', NAI (http://census. nationalarchives.ie/reels/nai002586687) (7 Apr. 2019).

30 Mark Rothery, 'Communities of kin and English landed gentry families of the nineteenth and early twentieth centuries', *Family and Community History*, 21:2 (2018), pp 112–28 at p. 124.

31 Death registration, George Mansfield, 5 Jan. 1929 (GRO) (www.irishgenealogy. ie) (7 Apr. 2019); Death Registration, Alice Mansfield, 12 Mar. 1934 (GRO) (www.irishgenealogy.ie) (7 Apr. 2019).

32 Eustace Mansfield, Morristown Lower, Kildare, Form A, 'Census of Ireland, 1901', NAI (http://census. nationalarchives.ie/reels/nai000912502) (30 June 2019); George Mansfield, Morristown Lower, Kildare, Form A, 'Census of Ireland, 1911', NAI (http:// census.nationalarchives.ie/reels/ nai002586687) (30 June 2019).

33 Le Play, *L'organisation de la famille*, pp 3–29.

34 Amanda Shanks, 'The Stem family reconsidered: the case of the minor gentry of Northern Ireland', *Journal of Comparative Family Studies*, 18:3 (1987), pp 352–6.

35 O'Neill, *Catholics of consequence*, p. 156.

36 Adam Kuper, 'Changing the subject: about cousin marriage, among other things', *Journal of the Royal Anthropological Institute*, 14:4 (2008), p. 721.

37 O'Neill, *Catholics of consequence*, p. 156.

38 *Burke's landed gentry of Ireland*, p. 450.

39 Rothery, 'Communities of kin', p. 124.

40 Kuper, 'Cousin marriage', p. 721.

41 Duffy, 'Colonial spaces', p. 23.

42 Eustace Lattin Mansfield Personal Papers, Marriage certificate (NLI, Mansfield Papers, MS 38, 431/2); *Burke's landed gentry of Ireland*, p. 457.

43 *Leicester Daily*, 27 Jan. 1911.

44 Marriage registration, Rosalind Mansfield and Hugh Sweetman, 17 Apr. 1941, GRO (www.irishgenealogy.ie) (9 June 2019).

45 *Leinster Express*, 18 Feb. 1905; *London Evening Standard*, 8 Jan. 1908; *Irish Independent*, 3 Nov. 1911; *Birmingham Daily Gazette*, 30 Oct. 1911.

46 LGB, *Return of owners*, p. 141 (www. failteromhat.com) (18 June 2019); *Irish Independent*, 15 Oct. 1912; *Kerry Evening Star*, 23 Dec. 1912; Landed estates database, Family Cronin (Park) (landedestates.nuigalway.ie) (8 Jun. 2019).

47 Shanks, 'Stem family reconsidered', p. 358.

48 Senia Pašeta, *Before the revolution: nationalism, social change and Ireland's Catholic elite, 1879–1922*, pp 33, 37.

49 Pašeta, *Before the revolution*, p. 37.

50 George and Alice Mansfield Personal correspondence (NLI, Mansfield Papers, MS 38, 418/7). This collection includes four letters written by an 11-year-old Eustace to his parents in 1890 while in Hodder Place, the preparatory school for Stonyhurst College: School notebooks of Henry Marie Lattin Mansfield (NLI, Mansfield Papers, MS 38, 429/1); English history notes written by Tirso Lattin Mansfield (NLI, Mansfield Papers, MS 38, 427/1).

51 O'Neill, *Catholics of consequence*, p. 133.

52 Ibid., pp 75–9.

53 Pašeta, *Before the revolution*, pp 38–9.

54 Rothery, 'Communities of kin', pp 684–5.

55 O'Neill, *Catholics of consequence*, p. 133.

56 Ibid., pp 108–9, 113.

57 Ibid., p. 156; *Prizes awarded to the scholars of Stonyhurst College* (1890–5), SCA, B2 (41). Note that Stonyhurst College does not publish or hold an archive that lists all students by year and thus has offered this publication as the closest approximation.

58 Letters to Alice Mansfield from Henry, 1890–1917 (NLI, Mansfield Papers, MS 38, 418/8).

59 O'Neill, *Catholics of consequence*, pp 132, 137–9.

60 Ibid., pp 113–15.

61 Ibid., p. 126.

62 Death registration, Captain Eustace Mansfield, 14 Apr. 1945 (GRO) (www. irishgenealogy.ie) (7 Apr. 2019); Revd Francis Irwin, *Stonyhurst war record*

(Derby, 1927); NLI, Mansfield Papers, Collection list 77.

2. CATHOLIC ELITE NETWORKS IN IRELAND THROUGH THE LENS OF GEORGE AND ALICE MANSFIELD

1   Costello, *A class apart*, p. 66.
2   Costello, *A class apart*, pp 66–7.
3   Letters from George Mansfield (NLI, Mansfield Papers, MS 38,409/1).
4   *Leinster Leader*, 11 Jan. 1890.
5   LGB, *Return of owners*, p. 154 (www.failteromhat.com) (18 June 2019).
6   Costello, *A class apart*, pp 82–90; LGB, *Return of owners*, p. 28 (www.failteromhat.com) (18 June 2019).
7   Alice Mansfield Diary (NLI, Mansfield Papers, MS 38,423/1), 13, 17 Aug. 1886.
8   NLI, Mansfield Papers, MS 38,423/1, 23 Apr. 1878, 7 May 1885, 26 Apr. 1887; *Leinster Express*, 27 Apr. 1878.
9   NLI, Mansfield Papers, MS 38,423/1, 26 Apr. 1878.
10 Costello, *A class apart*, pp 25–7.
11 Rothery, 'Communities of kin', pp 116–17.
12 GPL's great-great-grandmother was a Eustace and it would appear that Emma Eustace is a distant cousin living at Morristown Lattin. Emma is often mentioned by George in letters from France when she travelled with him and his sister in 1870–2, and seems to be considered almost as a sibling. She also wrote eight times to GPL between 1872 and 1881, with an 1881 letter speaking of GPL paying her a 'pension'.
13 LGB, *Return of owners*, p. 73 (www.failteromhat.com) (18 June 2019).
14 LGB, *Return of owners*, pp 65, 73 (www.failteromhat.com) (18 June 2019); Will of Elizabeth Paulina Thunder, Will registers of Ireland, 1858–91, NAI. From this will, it would appear that George and Eliza had twelve children living in 1878: *Freeman's Journal*, 21 Jan. 1875.
15 NLI, Mansfield Papers, MS 38,423/1, 15, 20 Feb. 1878.
16 Ibid., 26 Dec. 1879.
17 Ibid., 20 Dec. 1878, 1 Apr. 1882, 10 Mar. 1885.
18 Ibid., 5 May 1885.
19 Ibid., 23 Apr. 1887.
20 NLI, Mansfield Papers, MS 38,423/1, 28 Jan. 1878.

21 Ibid., 17 July 1878, 27 Nov. 1879.
22 Ibid., 3 Sept. 1879, 14 Feb. 1882.
23 *Wexford People*, 3 Jan. 1874; LGB, *Return of owners*, p. 94 (www.failteromhat.com) (18 June 2019).
24 The Cliffes are also mentioned in a letter George sent from France in 1872 to his father in Ireland, thus a part of their network in France too.
25 Ryan, 'Clongorey evictions', pp 73–4.
26 Ibid., p. 73.
27 Rothery, 'Communities of kin', pp 113–14.
28 Duffy, 'Colonial spaces', pp 21–2.
29 *Burke's landed gentry of Ireland*, pp 784–5; Appointments and awards (NLI, Mansfield Papers, MS 38,391/2–38,391/10); Ciaran O'Neill, 'Power, wealth and Catholic identity in Ireland, 1850–1900' in O.P. Rafferty (ed.), *Irish Catholic identities* (Manchester, 2013), pp 267–8.
30 *Leinster Leader*, 14 July 1883.
31 Thomas Nelson, 'Kildare County Council, 1899–1926' (PhD, NUIM, 2007), p. 41.
32 Murphy, 'Lady Charlotte Stopford', p. 228.
33 NLI, Mansfield Papers, MS 38,423/1, 27 Aug., 20 Oct. 1884.
34 *Kildare Observer*, 2 May 1891; *Journal of the Co. Kildare Archaeological Society*, 1891–5, i (Dublin, 1895), pp 1–2.
35 George Mansfield 1873 Diary (NLI, Mansfield Papers, MS 38,422/1).
36 Tom Hunt, *Sport and society in Victorian Ireland* (Cork, 2007), p. 14.
37 Costello, *A class apart*, p. 17.
38 Figure 14 shows a newspaper report from the *Leinster Express* in Jan. 1877 referencing GPL Mansfield and two of his brothers.
39 Irish Newspaper Archive (https://archive-irishnewsarchive-com.proxy.lib.ul.ie/) (2 June 2019).
40 Murphy, 'Lady Charlotte Stopford', p. 244.
41 Costello, *A class apart*, p. 19.
42 NLI, Mansfield Papers, MS 38,423/1, 6 Nov. 1879.
43 Costello, *A class apart*, p. 19.
44 *Leinster Express*, 19 Apr. 1879.
45 *Leinster Express*, 20 Dec. 1884; NLI, Mansfield Papers, MS 38,423/1, 9 Dec. 1884.

46 Hunt, *Sport and society*, p. 10.
47 Ibid., pp 76–8.
48 Ibid., pp 79, 82.
49 *Leinster Express*, 23 July 1881.
50 NLI, Mansfield Papers, MS 38,423/1, 11 Aug.–1 Sept. 1879.
51 Ibid., 2–5 Sept. 1879.

3. THE IMPACT OF ADDING A BI-NATIONAL DIMENSION TO AN IRISH CATHOLIC ELITE NETWORK

1   'Early history of the Thorn family of Long Island', *The New York Genealogical and Biographical Record*, 96:2 (New York, 1965), pp 96–7. Alice's parents had separated prior to 1869, subsequent to which her mother lived in New York with two of her siblings while her father lived in Paris with another of her siblings. Alice's mother died in New York in 1874, three years prior to Alice's marriage, following which it seems that all Alice's siblings were based in France.
2   Letters to Alice d'Audebard de Férussac from her mother, 1861–74 (NLI, Mansfield Papers, MS 38, 490/5).
3   Letters to Alice Mansfield from friends (NLI, Mansfield Papers, MS 38, 418/2).
4   Letters to Alice Mansfield from Henry, 1890–1917 (NLI, Mansfield Papers, MS 38, 418/8).
5   NLI, Mansfield Papers, MS 38,423/1, 29 July 1884, 29 June 1886, 29 Aug. 1885, 14 Sept. 1886, 15 Feb. 1878.
6   Rothery, 'Communities of kin', pp 119–20.
7   O'Riordan, 'Leisure with a purpose', p. 210.
8   MacKnight, 'Cake and conversation', p. 342.
9   Jessica Gerard, *County house life: family and servant, 1815–1914* (Oxford, 1995), p. 128.
10 Letters to Alice from friends (NLI, Mansfield Papers, MS 38, 418/2).
11 *Leinster Leader*, 21 Nov. 2014.
12 The methodology used here has drawn on that used within Murphy, 'Lady Charlotte Stopford', p. 229.
13 Karl Baedeker, *South-western France from the Loire and the Rhone to the Spanish frontier: handbook for travellers* (Leipsic, 1895), pp 68, 123–4; Alice's paternal grandmother lived in Pleurs, France, explaining Alice's three-day stay there in

1880, the last time they saw each other before her grandmother's death. Note that it is difficult to distinguish London in Figure 18 as the time spent there was only one day.
14 NLI, Mansfield Papers, MS 38,423/1, 19 Nov. 1883, 19 Dec. 1885.
15 Ibid., 18–21 May 1886.
16 NLI, Mansfield Papers, MS 38,423/1, 24 Mar., 17, 23 Apr. 1884.
17 Ibid., 27 May 1886.
18 Ibid., 3 Jan., 20, 27 Feb. 1886.
19 NLI, Mansfield Papers, MS 38,423/1, 28 Oct. 1885.
20 Ibid., 28 Nov.–7 Dec. 1885.
21 Ibid., 5–10 May 1886.
22 Ibid., 4, 19 Oct. 1878.
23 Ibid., 5, 16 June 1880.
24 NLI, Mansfield Papers, MS 38,423/1, 25–6 May 1880.
25 NLI, Mansfield Papers, MS 38,423/1, 27 Nov. 1883, 12 June 1885; profile for François André d'Audebard de Férussac, Geneanet (en.geneanet.org) (19 July 2019).
26 L.G.B., *Return of owners* (www.failteromhat.com) (18 July 2019); *Burke's peerage* (105th ed., London, 1980); *Debretts peerage, baronetage, knightage and companionage* (London, 1893), p. 286.
27 L.G.B., *Return of owners*, p. 148 (www.failteromhat.com) (18 July 2019); Matthew Potter, 'William Monsell: an Irish Catholic Unionist', *North Munster Antiquarian Journal*, 41 (2001), pp 70–1.
28 Potter, 'William Monsell', p. 73.
29 NLI, Mansfield Papers, MS 38,423/1, 1 Jan., 22 Feb., 3 May 1886.
30 Ibid., 9 Jan., 4 Feb. 1884.
31 *Belfast Newsletter*, 2 Sept. 1938.
32 *Belfast Newsletter*, 13 Apr. 1885.
33 L.G.B., *Return of owners*, p. 275 (www.failteromhat.com) (18 July 2019); *Burke's peerage* (105th ed., London, 1980), p. 525.
34 NLI, Mansfield Papers, MS 38,423/1, 19 Dec. 1885, 11 Feb. 1886.
35 *The complete peerage of England, Scotland, Ireland, Great Britain and the United Kingdom, extant, extinct or dormant*, III, ed. G.E. Cokayne and Vicary Gibbs (Gloucester, 2000), p. 139; Baedeker, *South-western France*, pp 68, 123–4.
36 A 1907 article in *Le Sport Universel Illustré*, 547 states that almost all the horses used

in the Biarritz hunt were Irish and
that the region of Biarritz was very
close to Ireland, with one gentleman
mentioned as travelling every year
to the Dublin Horse Show to
bring good horses back to
Biarritz.

37 *Le Sport Universel Illustré*, 3 Feb. 1907.

38 NLI, Mansfield Papers, MS 38,423/1, 12
Dec. 1883.

39 Death certificate, 7 Feb. 1885, Genealogy
society indexes (en.geneanet.org) (19 July
2019).

CONCLUSION

1 Dooley, *The decline of the big house*, p. 11.